DATE DUE

Measuring the Costs
of Protection
in Japan

YOKO SAZANAMI
SHUJIRO URATA
HIROKI KAWAI

Measuring the Costs
of Protection
in Japan

Institute for International Economics
Washington, DC
January 1995

) Sazanami is Professor of Economics
eio University in Tokyo and special-
in international trade and trade
.y. She is a member of the Council
Monetary System, Fiscal System
ncil, and the Economic Council to
Prime Minister. She has written both
 and journal articles, including
erminants of Japanese Foreign Direct
stment—Locational Attractiveness of
)pean Countries to Japanese Multina-
als" (*Revue Economique* May 1992).

iro Urata is Professor of Economics at
eda University in Tokyo. He was
ierly a Research Associate at the
)kings Institution and an Economist
ie World Bank. He is an author or
coauthor of numerous articles in
professional journals including the *Review
of Economics and Statistics*, *The Journal of
Development Economics*, *The Journal of
Comparative Economics*, and *The Mathematical Programming Study*. He has also
published a number of books on
international economic issues in Japanese.

Hiroki Kawai is a Research Associate at
the Japan Center for Economic Research
and specializes in consumer theory. He
received his master's degree in business
and commerce at Keio University. He can
be contacted at Fax no. 81-3-3639-2814.

INSTITUTE FOR INTERNATIONAL
ECONOMICS
11 Dupont Circle, NW
Washington, DC 20036-1207
(202) 328-9000   FAX: (202) 328-0900

C. Fred Bergsten, *Director*
Christine F. Lowry, *Director of Publications*

Cover design by Michelle M. Fleitz
Typesetting by Sandra F. Watts
Printing by Kirby Lithographic

Library of Congress Cataloging-in-
Publication Data

Sazanami, Yoko, 1932–
   Measuring the costs of protection in
Japan / Yoko Sazanami, Shujiro Urata,
Hiroki Kawai.
      p.   cm.
   The companion volume to Gary C.
Hufbauer and Kimberly Ann Elliott's
Measuring the costs of protection in the
United States, 1994.
   Includes bibliographical references.
   1. Protectionism—Japan. 2. Nontariff
trade barriers—Japan. 3. Competition,
Imperfect—Japan. 4. Protectionism—
United States. I. Urata, Shujiro, 1950–.
II. Kawai, Hiroki. III. Hufbauer, Gary
Clyde. Measuring the costs of protec-
tion in the United States. IV. Institute
for International Economics (U.S.)
V. Title.
HF2366.S29   1994
382'.73'0952—dc20   94-22349
                                      CIP

ISBN 0-88132-211-3

Marketed and Distributed outside the USA and Canada by Longman Group UK
Limited, London

The views expressed in this publication are those of the authors. This publication is
part of the overall program of the Institute, as endorsed by its Board of Directors,
but does not necessarily reflect the views of individual members of the Board or
the Advisory Committee.

Contents

Preface

The Institute has continually analyzed the impact of trade barriers on economies around the world. We have devoted particular attention to the situation in the United States, both in the aggregate (*Measuring the Costs of Protection in the United States*, 1994) and in key sectors (*The Future of World Trade in Textiles and Apparel*, revised 1990). We have also assessed the trade impact of international negotiations, most recently NAFTA (*NAFTA: An Assessment*, revised 1993) and the Uruguay Round under the GATT (*The Uruguay Round: An Assessment*, 1994).

As part of our extensive new program of studies of Asia Pacific economic cooperation, we will be conducting in-depth studies of the effects of trade barriers in a number of countries in the region. This analysis of Japan is the first in that series; it also relates to the Institute's ongoing work on trade relations between the United States and Japan, most recently in *Reconcilable Differences? United States–Japan Economic Conflict*, 1993. We hope that this new volume will provide both a better understanding of the magnitude of Japanese trade restraints and an indication of where future negotiations might best be directed.

We are particularly pleased that this study has been conducted by three leading Japanese economists. They worked closely with our own staff, and I would particularly thank Gary Hufbauer and Kimberly Ann Elliott for their extensive cooperation with our colleagues in Tokyo. International economic issues will increasingly require international scholarly cooperation, and we hope that this volume will indicate the benefits from such efforts.

The Institute for International Economics is a private nonprofit institution for the study and discussion of international economic policy. Its purpose is to analyze important issues in that area and to develop and communicate practical new approaches for dealing with them. The Institute is completely nonpartisan.

The Institute is funded largely by philanthropic foundations. Major institutional grants are now being received from the German Marshall Fund of the United States, which created the Institute with a generous commitment of funds in 1981, and from the Ford Foundation, the William and Flora Hewlett Foundation, the William M. Keck, Jr. Foundation, the Andrew Mellon Foundation, the C. V. Starr Foundation, and the United States–Japan Foundation. A number of other foundations and private corporations also contribute to the highly diversified financial resources of the Institute. The Dayton Hudson Foundation provides support for the Institute's program of studies on trade policy. The Center for Global Partnership provided partial support for this project. About 12 percent of the Institute's resources in our latest fiscal year were provided by contributors outside the United States, including about 5 percent from Japan.

The Board of Directors bears overall responsibility for the Institute and gives general guidance and approval to its research program— including identification of topics that are likely to become important to international economic policymakers over the medium run (generally, one to three years), and which thus should be addressed by the Institute. The Director, working closely with the staff and outside Advisory Committee, is responsible for the development of particular projects and makes the final decision to publish an individual study.

The Institute hopes that its studies and other activities will contribute to building a stronger foundation for international economic policy around the world. We invite readers of these publications to let us know how they think we can best accomplish this objective.

C. FRED BERGSTEN
Director
November 1994

Acknowledgments

This study was launched in the fall of 1991, when we received a letter from Gary Hufbauer and Kim Elliott inviting us to join their project on comparing the costs of protection in the United States, Europe and Japan. We would like to thank both of them for their advice, enthusiasm and above all patience in carefully checking our complicated estimation procedures and commenting on our manuscript. We would also like to thank C. Fred Bergsten, who gave us valuable comments and encouragement.

In addition, we would like to thank our colleagues in Japan, especially Iwao Tanaka who prepared the basic price indices. Keio Economic Observatory kindly provided us the space and facilities that enabled the three of us, who belong to different organizations, to work together.

1

Trade Protection in Japan

Critics of Japanese trade policy contend that, by insulating domestic industries from foreign competition, and by providing them a platform from which to export aggressively, the Japanese government enables domestic firms to gain valuable ground in the global race for industrial leadership. This study shows that significant import protection is discernible in a small fraction of Japanese industries. But interventionist Japanese policies are still seen as a major factor behind the success of key sectors, such as automobiles and electronics. Policies to protect and promote infant industries may be justified for a developing country, and thus were acceptable for Japan in the 1950s and 1960s. But they are viewed as acutely unfair when practiced by Japan today, when it is a rich industrial country.

Adding their small voices to the chorus of foreign criticism have been Japanese consumers, who are finally beginning to complain about the closed nature of the Japanese market. Some Japanese consumers now realize that the substantial yen appreciation of recent years has not been translated into lower prices for imported products, and that basic food and clothing are far more expensive in Tokyo than in New York.

The persistence of huge Japanese trade surpluses has further animated the controversy among politicians and economists, both within Japan and among its trading partners.[1] Japan's trade surplus declined in the early 1980s following the second oil crisis but increased sharply after

---

1. We use the term "trade surpluses" to refer only to merchandise trade. Japan generally runs a surplus in merchandise trade and now has a rough balance in services trade.

1985, to $130 billion in 1993. In years of slow worldwide growth, such as from 1990 to 1993, the Japanese trade surplus may reduce employment opportunities elsewhere in the world economy. This possibility causes a great deal of bilateral friction between Japan and its trading partners. Even in years of good worldwide growth, such as 1987–88, Japan's trade surpluses are criticized as the reflection of closed markets. Japan's trade surpluses are largely explained by macroeconomic variables—the exchange rate of the yen and differences in saving-investment balances between Japan and its trading partners. Nevertheless, critics of Japanese industrial and agricultural policies insist that protection must be listed among the causes.

There is another cause for complaint within Japan and from a global welfare perspective about Japanese protection. Barriers on imports essentially work as a tax on exports. In practical terms, the high costs paid by Japanese consumers for food, beverages, textiles, and other manufactured articles translate both into higher average wage costs for Japanese firms and into a stronger yen. Protection for industrial materials such as fuels, metals, and chemicals also raises input costs for other Japanese firms. The predictable result is that Japanese exporters are less competitive in world markets. In some situations, import protection can serve instead as export promotion (see Krugman 1984), but that does not appear to be the case in the large majority of sectors studied here.

These controversies over Japan's trade policy motivate our study. But rather than examining the long-run global consequences of Japan's industrial and agricultural policies, or cataloging the reasons for persistent Japanese trade surpluses, we focus on the microeconomic underpinnings of trade protection.[2] We aim to assess the level of protection enjoyed by Japanese industry and agriculture and to evaluate its immediate impact on the Japanese economy.

The highlights of our findings may be briefly summarized. We conclude that Japanese tariff and nontariff barriers inflicted a cost on Japanese consumers of ¥10 trillion to ¥15 trillion in 1989 ($75 billion to $110 billion at the 1989 exchange rate of ¥138 to the dollar). At the expense of consumers, Japanese producers pocketed perhaps ¥7 trillion to ¥9.6 trillion ($50 billion to $70 billion). The Japanese government collected only around ¥0.3 trillion ($2 billion) in tariff revenue. The net cost to Japanese society as a whole amounted to somewhere between ¥1.1 trillion and ¥2.4 trillion (between $8 billion and $17 billion). The results are presented in table 3.3 and explained in chapter 3.

In Japan, protection from imported goods is confined to agriculture and a small number of manufacturing industries, but some of these are

---

2. For an examination of the long-run global consequences of Japan's policies, see Bergsten and Noland (1993).

very highly protected indeed. The tariff-equivalent rates averaged 178 percent for these highly protected sectors of Japanese agriculture and industry. The aggregate cost to Japanese consumers in these sectors was in the range of 2.6 to 3.8 percent of GNP. If all the implied barriers had been removed, 1989 Japanese imports of highly protected products might have increased by as much ¥7.3 trillion (more than $50 billion). Complete liberalization of Japanese markets would not, however, reduce Japan's trade surplus by this extent. Instead, the reallocation of resources within Japan and downward pressure on the yen would increase exports by nearly the same amount as the gain in imports.

The significant appreciation of the Japanese yen between 1989 and 1993, from ¥138 to ¥112 to the dollar, meant that imports were about 20 percent cheaper, in yen terms, in 1993 than 1989. However, Japanese wholesale prices did not, on average, decline during this period. By implication, Japanese nontariff import barriers probably exert a greater protective effect today than they did in 1989, the year under study. The exceptions are a few food products, including beef and beef products, citrus, some dairy products, and some canned or bottled fruits and vegetables, where quotas have been liberalized in recent years.

Methods of Estimating Trade Protection

As other studies have done, we express levels of Japanese protection as tariff-equivalent duty rates. However, our method of estimating the level of protection differs sharply from two approaches often used in other studies. One common approach is to identify formal trade barriers, notably tariffs and quotas, and then to estimate their impact on the domestic price of the affected import and its competing domestic substitute (see, for example, Hufbauer and Elliott 1994).

Application of the Hufbauer-Elliott methodology to evaluate protection in Japan would encounter a severe problem. It is widely believed that Japanese markets are protected not only by formal tariffs and quotas, but also by nontransparent government barriers and by informal, nongovernmental barriers. If this is so, a method that focused on formal barriers would miss the biggest part of the Japanese story.

A second approach commonly used in prior studies is to survey the retail prices of the same commodities in different countries, to use these data to measure the extent of price differentials, and then to attribute the price differences to various barriers, including inefficient distribution systems within a country (see, for example, US Department of Commerce 1989, Organization for Economic Cooperation and Development 1992, Ministry of Agriculture, Fishery, and Forestry 1992, and Ministry of International Trade and Industry [MITI] 1992). In the survey method, the price of a given television set in Japan might be compared with the price of the same set in the United States. To the extent the television set is priced higher in Japan than the United States, the differential is attributed to a combination of Japanese government protection, private restrictive practices by Japanese firms, and inefficient Japanese distribution systems. Survey studies generally experience at least two problems: an inability to find commodities of comparable characteristics sold in two or more countries and an inability to distinguish price differentials caused by dissimilar distribution systems from those caused by differing levels of protection.

Our study, unlike prior scholarly work, directly compares c.i.f. import unit values (i.e., the unit value in Japanese ports, before tariffs or any markup by domestic wholesalers) with domestic producers' unit values (i.e., the ex-factory or ex-farm unit value before markup by domestic wholesalers). Unit values are calculated by dividing the declared value of imports, or the value of producers' shipments, by the number of discrete units or by the appropriate physical unit of measure (kilograms, yards, etc.).

The use of unit values enables comparisons across a much wider range of commodity categories than is possible with price surveys, because unit values are readily available for a large number of products. The unit value method should, in principle, capture the impact of informal governmental and nongovernmental barriers, as well as the effect of tariffs and quotas. In both these respects, the potential scope of our method extends beyond the scope of approaches previously used. On the other hand, unit value comparisons are plagued with statistical difficulties. Later we discuss these difficulties and illustrate how they qualify our results.

Because unit value comparisons are subject to statistical problems, the implied level of protection for a single good, or even several goods in a category, must be viewed with caution. An example illustrates our approach. If the unit value of an imported good is 100 and the unit value of its domestic counterpart is 150, the comparison suggests that the domestic industry receives tariff-equivalent protection equal to 50 percent of the imported unit value. If the statutory tariff is a lesser figure, say 5 percent, the remaining gap (45 percent) may be attributed to quantitative restrictions or to other, less transparent barriers. But other explanations are certainly possible, the principal one being quality differences between the domestic and the imported product per physical unit. Nevertheless, we believe that unit value differentials across a range of commodity categories roughly indicate the extent of formal and informal protection. This is a key assumption of our study. Later we perform sensitivity tests that lend some degree of confidence to our approach. However, readers who believe that quality differences provide the dominant explanation for unit value differentials will disagree with most of the analysis that follows.

Assuming, as we do, that unit value differentials often reflect protective barriers, we can then use them to assess the impact of protection on consumers, producers, and importers in Japan. These calculations are carried out in chapter 3.

Calculating Unit Value Differentials

Appendix A discusses in detail the construction of unit values. Here we explain the derivation of the key element in our analysis—namely, the unit value differentials for 1989. The calculated differentials are shown in table 1.1, expressed as tariff equivalents. These are calculated as 100 times the difference between the producers' unit value Pd and the import unit value Pm, divided by the import unit value, or:

$$100 \times [(Pd - Pm)/Pm]_{89} \qquad (1.1)$$

where the subscript "89" indicates that this is the tariff equivalent for 1989. The addendum to this chapter compares this method of evaluating the tariff equivalent of tariff and nontariff barriers with the price survey method.

To begin constructing the tariff-equivalent figures, we obtained 1985 c.i.f. import data from official trade statistics (Japan Tariff Association 1985) and 1985 domestic production data from the 1985 Japanese input-output table (Management and Coordination Agency 1989). In order to bring 1985 unit value differentials calculated from this data forward to 1989, we used domestic producers' price indices from the MITI 1985 and 1989 input-output tables and import price indices derived from 1985 and 1989 c.i.f. import statistics.

The unit value differentials had to be calculated for a wide variety of goods, which we categorized in three levels, ranging from the specific to the general: "items," "commodities," and "product categories." Where possible, we started by calculating a unit value differential between a specific domestic item and a set of similar imported products to create a commodity-level unit value differential. In some cases, closely related domestic items were grouped and a unit value calculated using quantity weights. That domestic unit value was then compared to a similarly constructed unit value for a set of closely related import items to get a commodity-level unit value differential. Similar commodities were next grouped together into a product category, which corresponds to a category in the input-output table. The commodity-level differentials were combined, using value weights, to calculate the unit value differential for the input-output product category. The results in this study are reported at the product category level.

In some product categories, all the individual items were similar (for

Table 1.1 Unit value differentials, tariff and nontariff barrier rates, imports, domestic production, and import penetration, 1989[a] (percentages unless noted otherwise)

Sector and product category	Unit value differential[b]	Tariff rate[c]	Implied nontariff barrier rate[d]	Imports (billions of 1989 yen)	Annual growth in imports, 1985–89[e]	Domestic production (billions of 1989 yen)	Import penetration[f]
Food and beverages	**280.7**	**8.2**	**272.5**	**2,000**	**6.0**	**19,311**	**9.4**
Wheat	477.8	0.0	477.8	164	−9.0	162	50.3
Soybeans	423.6	0.0	423.6	185	−11.2	60	75.5
Citrus fruits	128.5	14.1	114.4	79	1.1	290	21.4
Oilseeds other than soybeans	628.6	0.0	628.6	83	−10.1	1	99.3
Leaf tobacco	119.6	0.0	119.6	3	28.0	136	2.2
Dressed carcasses (beef, pork, etc.) and poultry	38.6	14.1	24.5	622	11.5	1,931	24.4
Processed meat products	119.8	17.9	101.9	31	16.1	835	3.5
Dairy products	228.6	17.6	211.0	83	7.0	483	14.7
Milled rice	737.1	0.0	737.1	2	−2.4	3,040	0.1
Bread	346.5	6.5	340.0	1	11.7	1,008	0.1
Confectionery goods	210.8	18.8	192.0	58	10.3	1,226	4.5
Canned or bottled vegetables and fruits	139.2	18.0	121.2	93	4.3	379	19.6
Beer	143.0	1.7	141.3	24	41.1	2,294	1.0
Whiskey and brandy	94.1	5.9	88.2	291	16.4	469	38.3
Tea and roasted coffee	718.4	11.9	706.5	19	−4.7	599	3.1
Sparkling and still beverages	197.0	17.1	179.9	27	56.1	2,383	1.1
Tobacco products	241.2	0.0	241.2	237	21.9	4,015	5.6
Textiles and light industries	**102.5**	**11.0**	**91.5**	**1,364**	**20.9**	**4,983**	**21.5**
Cotton yarn	39.6	5.3	34.3	84	−4.7	337	19.9
Knit fabrics	8.1	8.1	0.0	451	19.8	1,256	26.4
Clothing	292.6	10.4	282.2	567	25.0	1,351	29.6
Plywood	30.7	11.6	19.1	159	56.1	995	13.7
Paper	22.1	3.3	18.8	73	13.7	874	7.7
Leather footwear	13.8	6.4	7.4	31	18.6	170	15.3
Metal products	**59.5**	**0.8**	**58.7**	**1197**	**1.1**	**2,119**	**36.1**
Copper ore	159.2	0.0	159.2	261	4.6	3	98.9
Sheet glass	63.1	1.3	61.8	37	24.4	673	5.2

Clay refractories	180.3	1.2	179.1	9	0.2	385	2.3
Ferroalloys	21.6	3.5	18.1	178	7.8	239	42.6
Lead (incl. regenerated)	23.4	3.5	19.9	9	−5.3	62	12.2
Regenerated aluminum	25.9	0.8	25.1	174	18.0	551	24.0
Other nonferrous metals	13.5	0.4	13.1	530	−3.4	205	72.1
Chemical products	**128.3**	**1.4**	**126.9**	**1,356**	**−11.8**	**12,088**	**10.1**
Natural gas	113.4	0.0	113.4	770	−20.5	78	90.7
Nitric fertilizers	84.8	0.0	84.8	6	29.6	40	13.2
Soda ash	148.5	0.0	148.5	7	−1.5	47	12.3
Caustic soda	223.7	4.9	218.8	1	24.3	192	0.8
Titanium oxide	39.8	4.1	35.7	20	10.5	106	15.6
Methane derivatives	193.0	2.3	190.7	38	−2.9	144	20.8
Industrial oil and fat	44.7	0.8	43.9	11	−3.4	74	13.1
Polyethylene	33.2	5.7	27.5	32	10.9	1,356	2.3
Pharmaceuticals	8.5	3.4	5.1	395	4.9	5,552	6.6
Cosmetics, toilet preparations	661.6	2.0	659.6	55	18.3	837	6.1
Gasoline	229.0	5.5	223.5	21	35.6	3,663	0.6
Machinery	**140.2**	**0.3**	**139.9**	**1,274**	**12.2**	**15,511**	**7.6**
Chemical machinery	61.1	0.1	61.0	59	5.0	1,142	4.9
Radio and television sets	607.0	0.0	607.0	44	53.8	1,022	4.1
Electric computing equipment	75.8	0.0	75.8	574	10.6	6,384	8.2
Communication equipment	236.6	0.1	236.5	80	10.2	2,723	2.9
Semiconductor devices	106.6	0.0	106.6	358	14.1	3,515	9.3
Medical instruments	32.7	2.1	30.6	158	13.8	724	17.9
Total for listed products	**178.2**	**4.7**	**173.5**	**7,191**	**3.6**	**54,013**	**11.7**

a. Source data, at the item and the commodity level, for this and all tables in this study may be obtained from Hiroki Kawai (see page iv). Figures for sectors and totals for all listed products are value-weighted averages of the product categories they contain using import values or the sum of import and domestic production values as appropriate.

b. The unit value differential for 1989 is defined by equation (1.2) in the text and interpreted as a rough measure of the tariff equivalent of tariffs and nontariff barriers.

c. Realized ad valorem tariff rate.

d. Calculated as the unit value differential minus the realized ad valorem tariff rate.

e. At constant 1985 prices.

f. Defined as: import volume/(domestic production + import volume). No account is taken of exports which are small for most of these products.

Sources: Unit value differentials are from appendix A. All other data are from the Japanese input-output tables (Management and Coordination Agency 1989, and MITI various years).

7

example, the three tariff line items for imported wheat). Hence these items formed the only commodity group in that product category. In such cases, a product category unit value was obtained simply by dividing the sum of the import values for individual items by the sum of the import volumes for those items to get a single unit value for both the commodity group and the product category. This unit value was then compared to the unit value for domestically produced wheat (a product category also composed of a single commodity group) to calculate the unit value differential (and thus the tariff equivalent) for the category.

For product categories comprising more heterogeneous products, the procedure for estimating unit value differentials was more complicated. For example, in the canned or bottled vegetables and fruits category there were five specific domestic product items that had to be matched to 42 import product items. The matching exercise yielded five separate commodity groups. Once this was done, a unit value differential was calculated for each of the five groups. Each commodity group differential was then weighted by its 1985 consumption value, and the weighted commodity group differentials in a particular category were added together to calculate a single 1985 product category unit value differential for canned and bottled fruits and vegetables.

The next step was to calculate *1989* unit value differentials for each product category, starting with the corresponding *1985* unit value differentials. The basic method may be described as follows:

$$100 \times [(Pd - Pm)/Pm]_{89} =$$
$$100 \times [Pd/Pm]_{85} \times [Pd(M^*89)/Pm(1^*89)] - 100 \qquad (1.2)$$

where:

$[Pd/Pm]_{85}$ = the 1985 ratio between domestic and import unit values for the product category

$Pd(M^*89)$ = the 1989 domestic price index calculated by MITI for the product category (where the 1985 index = 1.000)

$Pm(1^*89)$ = our preferred version of the 1989 import price index for the product category (where the 1985 index = 1.000); this preferred version is explained in appendix A.

In other words, to obtain the 1989 unit value differential, the 1985 unit value differential for a product category was adjusted upward if the domestic price index rose more (or fell less) than the import price index. Conversely, the 1985 unit value differential was adjusted downward if the domestic index rose less (or fell more) than the import price index.

We took the domestic price indices for each product category from MITI input-output tables. These indices were computed by MITI using base-year (1985) value weights for individual items. Similarly, we made our own calculations of the 1989 import price indices for each product category by applying 1985 value weights to changes in unit values for individual commodities within the product category.

To select our universe of protected categories, namely, the products listed in table 1.1, the following criteria were first applied to 1985 data:

- a minimum level of imports of ¥1 billion; and

- a minimum unit value differential between imports and competing domestic products of 5 percent.

The products that met the criteria for 1985 were screened again using 1989 data.[3]

In addition to the products selected by applying these criteria, a few products that have been the objects of trade controversy were examined, even though they did not meet the minimum unit value differential test. These products are citrus fruits, knit fabrics, paperboard, leather footwear, sheet glass, "other" nonferrous metals, chemical machinery, agricultural machinery, pharmaceuticals, and medical instruments (see table A.1).

Imports were registered in 420 categories in the 1985 input-output table, and 43 of these categories passed the 5 percent unit value differential criterion. Significantly, this implies that import protection in excess of the 5 percent differential was found for only 10 percent by count of import categories. Measured by import value, the selected categories are somewhat more important: they account for about 19 percent of the value of imports in 1989. However, their relative importance in terms of domestic production and employment was decidedly less: 7.0 and 3.2 percent by count and by value, respectively, in 1989.

It is useful to make a broad comparison between our calculated tariff equivalents, shown in the first column of table 1.1, and the price differential estimates made in other studies.[4] Although detailed comparisons are not warranted because of sharp differences in methodology, it is possible to assess the overall tenor of the various studies. This is done in table 1.2 for selected products. Generally, our calculated tariff equivalents greatly exceed the price differentials found by other scholars.

Unlike other studies, which compare prices at the retail level in different countries (including both wholesale and retail margins), our study

---

3. This method of selection will miss products that had a low differential in 1985 but a differential of 5 percent or more in 1989. Where other evidence suggested that the 1989 differentials might exceed our 5 percent threshold, we included the product category on a trial basis in appendix table A.1.

4. It should be noted that preliminary versions of table 1.1 have been published elsewhere (e.g., Bergsten and Noland 1993, 184). For some product categories the figures in table 1.1 differ significantly from these preliminary estimates.

Table 1.2 Price and unit value differentials from selected surveys (percentages)

Items[a]	Unit value differentials, ex-factory or ex-farm 1989 (this study)[b]	Tokyo versus New York retail, 1991[c]					PPP exchange rate, 1990 (OECD)[d]
		EPA	MOA	MITI (A)	MITI (B)	TA	
Citrus fruits	128.5	73.6 (oranges)					37.5
Milled rice	737.1		138.0				
Confectionery goods	210.8						59.3
Bread	346.5	−22.0	−15.0				59.3
Other sugar and by-products	0.0	61.6 (sugar) −19.0 (chocolate)	19.0 (sugar) 12.3 (chocolate)				99.6
Tea and roasted coffee	718.4	49.5	75.0 (tea) 49.0 (instant coffee)				46.3
Dairy products	228.6		75.0 (milk) 2.0 (yogurt)				29.2
Processed meat products	119.8	175.5 (100 g of beef)	244.8 (100 g of beef)				27.5

Clothing	292.6	26.9 (shirt) −31.0 (skirt)			72.4 (jeans)	177.8
Cosmetics	661.6			117.3 (lipstick)	0.1
Radio and television sets	607.0		−0.03 (color TV) −20.0 (color TV^e)		−27.0
Gasoline	229.0	74.6			60.6
Leather footwear	13.8	−17.4 (for men)			
Whiskey and brandy	94.1			63.8	129.8

EPA = Economic Planning Agency of Japan; MOA = Ministry of Agriculture; TA = Tax Agency; MITI(A) = Ministry of International Trade and Industry, products from Japan sold in New York and in Tokyo; MITI(B) = Ministry of International Trade and Industry, products from the United States sold in Tokyo and in New York; OECD = Organization for Economic Cooperation and Development, purchasing power parity (PPP) study.

a. Items listed in the table are those for which comparable price data are available.

b. The figures show price differentials, in the Japanese marketplace, as $(Pd − Pm)/Pm$, where Pd is the domestic Japanese producer's price and Pm is the c.i.f. import price.

c. All Tokyo *versus* New York retail figures represent the ratio $(Pt − Pny)/Pny$, where Pt is the retail price in Tokyo and Pny is the retail price in New York.

d. These figures can be interpreted as the percentage by which Japanese domestic prices are higher (or lower) than world prices translated at the 1990 exchange rate.

e. Discount store price.

Sources: Table 1.1, this study; Economic Planning Agency of Japan 1992, various tables; OECD 1992; authors' calculations.

compares Japanese domestic producers' unit values with Japanese c.i.f. unit values. However, the analysis in the addendum to this chapter suggests that the retail price method does not *necessarily* yield a different conclusion from that offered by our ex-factory (or ex-farm) method. A more likely explanation for the differing results shown in table 1.2 is that our study is based on unit values of items that may be highly dissimilar, whereas other surveys compare prices of identical or highly similar items. Because the Japanese item is generally (but not always) up-market compared with the import in cases where differences exist, this factor is likely to exaggerate the size of unit value differentials obtained here by comparison with retail price differentials found in other studies.[5] The next section examines this question in greater detail.

Sensitivity Analysis of Unit Value Differentials

To a large degree, observed unit value differentials may reflect an inexact matching between domestic products and imports. As already explained, unit value differentials are estimated by comparing the unit values of domestically produced goods with the unit values of similar imports. The use of unit values gives rise to inaccurate comparisons when the commodities in question have distinct product characteristics and differ in quality. For example, radio and television sets produced in Japan are generally expensive and of high quality, whereas imported sets are generally cheap and of low quality. Thus, unit value differentials for radio and television sets largely reflect product type and quality differences. The more general problem of type and quality differences, and therefore of comparisons based on unit prices, is acute for complex manufactured products such as electronic goods and machinery; it is not so severe for agricultural, mineral products, and basic chemicals.

Our sensitivity analysis attempts to probe the boundaries of these difficulties. Specifically, we postulate that commodity groups in the same product category should exhibit roughly similar unit value differentials, on the argument that governmental and nongovernmental barriers are likely to exert about the same degree of restrictiveness on similar commodities. Hence sharply dissimilar differentials for commodity groups within the same product category could suggest the existence of type and quality differences that bias the corresponding differentials upward.

Common sense suggests that the most plausible way to aggregate unit value differentials for a product category is to weight the differential for

---

5. Product categories where imports may instead be of generally higher quality than Japanese goods, per physical unit, include whiskey and brandy, pharmaceuticals, and medical instruments. For example, Scotch whiskey made in Scotland is probably of better quality than Scotch whiskey made in Japan.

each commodity group by the group's value share in the category. However, the calculation of an alternatively weighted differential may provide some indication of the existence of dissimilar types and qualities.

Suppose that, in a product category composed of two commodity groups, type and quality differences cause one commodity group to exhibit a sharply higher differential than the other. Also suppose that the commodity groups do not account for equal value shares in the category. In this case, the simple average of the commodity group differentials will differ from the value-weighted average; if the commodity group with the upward-biased differential has a majority value share, then the value-weighted average will exceed the simple average, and vice versa. In general, when product category differentials are highly sensitive to the weighting scheme, type and quality differences may play an important role in the observed differentials.

Based on this hypothesis, we have devised sensitivity tests to determine the extent to which simple-average weighting of commodity differentials alters the computed aggregate differentials for each product category, by comparison with value weighting for commodity differentials.[6] Appendix A explains the derivation and application of the sensitivity analysis in detail. Here we report only the main conclusions concerning the sensitivity of the 1989 unit value differentials to the use of alternative weighting methods.

First, we calculated for each product category the 1985 domestic unit value relative to the 1985 import unit value (Pd/Pm); in this comparison, unit values for both domestic goods and imported goods were computed using value weights. We then recalculated the relative levels using product category unit values based on simple averages. Next we calculated the ratios between the value-weighted relative levels and the simple-average relative levels. After that we extended the 1985 ratios forward to 1989 using different weighting schemes for the import price deflator (the schemes are explained in appendix A). Finally, we characterized the resulting 1989 ratios as belonging to one of four grades.

If the 1989 ratio was less than 0.75 or greater than 1.33, we characterized the calculated unit value differential as highly unstable. The implication is that type and quality differences may be a major cause of the observed differential. If the ratio was between 0.75 and 0.85, or between 1.18 and 1.33, we characterized the differential as moderately unstable. If the ratio was between 0.85 and 0.95, or between 1.05 and 1.18, we characterized it as moderately stable. Finally, if the ratio was between 0.95

---

6. With more time and resources, other sensitivity tests might have been applied. For example, the sensitivity of weighting at an item level rather than at a commodity level could have been explored. Preliminary analysis suggests, for example, that there is a high degree of instability at the item level for communications equipment and semiconductors.

and 1.05, we characterized it as highly stable. In this last case, the implication is that type and quality differences may not be very important.

The results of this sensitivity analysis, reported in table A.3, are as follows:

- Highly unstable 1989 unit value differentials: two product categories, accounting for 8.0 percent of 1989 imports in the product categories listed in table 1.1.

- Moderately unstable 1989 unit value differentials: five product categories, accounting for 9.5 percent of 1989 imports in the product categories listed in table 1.1.

- Moderately stable 1989 unit value differentials: seven product categories, accounting for 9.1 percent of 1989 imports in the product categories listed in table 1.1.

- Highly stable 1989 unit value differentials: seven product categories, accounting for 30 percent of 1989 imports in the product categories listed in table 1.1.

This summary excludes 26 product categories that were made up of a single commodity so that weighting schemes at the commodity level were not relevant. It also excludes the five product categories listed in table A.3 that did not pass the 1989 screen for a high level of implied protection. For the remaining categories, our sensitivity analysis suggests that the calculated differentials for 1989 are relatively robust across a variety of weighting methods, since 14 out of 21 categories can be characterized as highly or moderately stable. This finding suggests that quality and type differences may not be pervasive in the products covered by our data. However, since our sensitivity tests did not cover more than 40 percent of listed imports (belonging to the 26 omitted product categories) and since we did not explore a variety of other possible sensitivity tests, our conclusion can only be suggestive.

ADDENDUM: Comparison of Ex-Factory and Retail Methodologies for Computing Unit Value Differentials

Unit value differentials can be measured at two different levels: the ex-factory or ex-farm level, and the retail level. Measurement at the retail level incorporates markups for wholesale and retail distribution.

Ex-Factory or Ex-Farm Methodology

Japanese firms sell a certain product, ex-farm or ex-factory, at a unit value of Pd. The comparable imported product arrives at the Japanese border at a unit value of Pm, which includes transport expenses to reach Japan. Tariffs and nontariff barriers are then imposed. The ad valorem equivalents of these barriers may be added to Pm to give a landed unit value of Pm':

$$Pm' = Pm(1 + t + nt) \qquad (1)$$

where t is the ad valorem equivalent of tariffs and nt is the ad valorem equivalent of nontariff barriers.

If the domestic and imported products are genuinely equivalent, market forces should ensure that:

$$Pd = Pm'. \qquad (2)$$

Hence, by arithmetic, the inferred extent of tariff and nontariff barriers can be calculated as:

$$(Pd - Pm)/Pm = t + nt. \qquad (3)$$

Equation (3) is the key measure used in our study to assess the combined level of tariff and nontariff barriers.

Retail Methodology

Wholesalers and retailers who distribute Japanese products charge a combined markup, expressed as a percentage of the ex-factory or ex-farm unit value, of dd. By adding dd to the ex-factory or ex-farm unit value, it is possible to calculate the consumer unit value for the domestic product, Pdr:

$$Pdr = Pd(1 + dd). \qquad (4)$$

Wholesalers and retailers who distribute imports charge a combined markup of dm. By adding dm to the import unit value, it is likewise possible to calculate the consumer unit value for the imported product, Pmr:

$$Pmr = Pm'(1 + dm). \qquad (5)$$

Again, if domestic and imported products are equivalent, market forces should ensure that:

$$Pdr = Pmr = Pj, \qquad (6)$$

where Pj is the retail unit value in Japan for the product. Let Pus be the retail unit value for the same product in the United States, including wholesaler and retailer markups. The retail unit value differential between Japan and the United States can then be expressed as:

$$(Pj - Pus)/Pus. \qquad (7)$$

Equation (7) is the measure of protection used in survey studies of retail markets.

Comparison of Ex-Factory and Retail Methodologies

The two methodologies need not necessarily give the same result, but they are systematically related. The retail unit value of the product in the United States, Pus, is the ex-factory or ex-farm unit value, $Pusd$, plus wholesaler and retailer markups, dus:

$$Pus = Pusd(1 + dus). \qquad (8)$$

Assuming that Japanese imports come from the United States, the Japanese retail unit value, Pj, can be expressed as the US ex-factory or ex-farm unit value combined with three add-on costs: transport costs, tariff and nontariff barriers, and Japanese distribution margins:

$$Pj = Pusd(1 + cif)(1 + t + nt)(1 + dm). \qquad (9)$$

In equation (9), cif represents trans-Pacific transport costs (including insurance), expressed as a percentage of the US ex-factory unit value, incurred in shipping the product from the United States to Japan.

By arithmetic, the retail unit value differential is then:

$$(Pj - Pus)/Pus = \{[(1 + t + nt)(1 + cif)(1 + dm)]/(1 + dus)\} - 1 \qquad (10)$$

Equations (3) and (10) are equal if:

$$(1 + cif)(1 + dm) = (1 + dus) \qquad (11)$$

If the product of one plus the transport costs and one plus the Japanese distribution margins equals one plus the US distribution margins, then the ex-factory (or ex-farm) unit value differential will just equal the retail unit value differential. However, if Japanese distribution margins substantially exceed US margins, then the retail unit value differential will substantially exceed the ex-factory (or ex-farm) unit value differential. Only if Japanese distribution margins are much smaller than US distribution margins (which seems unlikely) would the retail unit value differential be much smaller than the ex-factory (or ex-farm) differential.

It should be stressed that several other factors frequently cited as contributing to relatively high retail prices in Japan, such as high land prices, an inefficient distribution system, and restrictive business practices among retailers, do not affect the ex-factory or ex-farm differentials studied here.

2

Japanese Policies and Practices Affecting Imports

Broadly speaking, two types of measures, tariffs and nontariff measures, protect domestic producers in Japan. Although tariff rates are relatively high for food and beverages (8.2 percent on average) and textiles and light industrial products (11.0 percent on average), rates are almost zero for other categories. The tariff rates shown in table 1.1 are realized ad valorem rates, computed as the ratio between tariff revenue and the c.i.f. value of imports, both taken from the 1989 input-output table (Ministry of International Trade and Industry 1992). The figures reflect both true ad valorem tariffs and specific duties (the latter are applied to several agricultural and mineral products). These realized tariff rates in many cases differ from the tariff rates bound under the General Agreement on Tariffs and Trade (GATT), because the realized rates reflect various special tariff arrangements. The special arrangements include the Generalized System of Preferences (GSP), seasonal tariffs applied to some agricultural products such as oranges, and differentiated tariff rates under tariff-quota systems applied to some agricultural products, such as oats, maize, and cheese.

Since unit value differentials for Japanese imports far exceed Japanese tariff rates, it seems likely that nontariff measures are a more substantial cause of protection in Japan than tariffs. Using our approach, implied nontariff barrier rates are calculated as the unit value differentials minus realized ad valorem tariff rates. These are shown in table 1.1. Examples of nontariff measures include import quotas and other overt import restrictions, government procurement limited to domestically produced goods, price support programs coupled with restrictions on domestic sales, and various restrictions stemming from the Japanese system of industrial organization.

The importance of nontariff barriers is illustrated by Japan's recent experience with yen appreciation. From an average of ¥242 to the dollar during 1985, the yen rose in value to ¥138 to the dollar during 1989. During this period, domestic wholesale prices for nonregulated products declined sharply, by about 22 percent, following the downward course of comparable import prices, which dropped about 26 percent. But domestic wholesale prices of regulated products declined on average only about 8 percent, despite a 25 percent decline in comparable import prices (Economic Planning Agency of Japan 1993, 162).

In the following sections, we outline for each agricultural and industrial sector listed in table 1.1 the various public policies and private practices that impede access to the Japanese market.

Food and Beverages

Japan is the world's largest food importer. Imports of food (Standard International Trade Classifications O and 1) amounted to ¥4.6 trillion in 1990 ($31.5 billion at then-current exchange rates). Nevertheless, food and beverages are the most heavily protected sectors in the Japanese economy. Import quotas at present restrict imports in 12 product categories. Of these, the only category listed in table 1.1 is dairy products; the other products did not meet our selection criteria. The price support system, which is designed to stabilize prices and supply and to provide guaranteed income levels for farmers, applies to a number of agricultural industries, among them soybean production, which is included in table 1.1. To achieve purposes similar to those of the price support system, the government operates state trading monopolies for eight products, including three listed in table 1.1: milled rice, wheat, and dairy products. The others (barley, salt, opium, alcohol, and raw silk) did not meet our selection criteria.

In table 1.1 a total of 27 products show calculated tariff equivalents greater than 100 percent, meaning that domestic producers' unit values for these products are more than twice as high as the corresponding import unit values. Of these 27 products, 15 are agricultural goods. This reflects a well-known phenomenon: Japan gives substantially more protection to agricultural products than to industrial products. These agricultural policies are designed to ensure food security and stable prices (rice and wheat), to stabilize farm income (dairy and meat), to promote a structural shift to new crops (fruit and vegetables), and to maintain farm income parity (sugar).

In our study, 17 items in the food and beverage categories passed the minimum 5 percent unit value differential criterion for 1989. The average unit value differential for these items was 281 percent in 1989 (table 1.1). High unit value differentials were already apparent in 1985 (see appendix A, table A.1). Subsequently, the 42 percent appreciation of the yen between 1985 and 1989 caused a decline of 24 percent in import prices for highly protected food and beverage products (calculated from table A.2). Meanwhile, domestic prices of these products only declined by 7 percent (also calculated from table A.2). The different patterns of import and domestic price behavior further increased unit value differentials between 1985 and 1989. Japan's public and private barriers apparently prevented the fall in yen import prices from exerting a comparable effect on domestic prices, and the average unit value differential for highly protected food and beverage products rose from 204 percent in 1985 to 281 percent in 1989.

Until the poor harvest of 1993 pushed the government to allow rice imports, the Japanese policy of self-sufficiency meant a virtual ban on rice imports.[1] The Organization for Economic Cooperation and Development (OECD) estimated the subsidy to Japanese rice producers at ¥2.7 trillion in 1990, or $19 billion (OECD 1992, based on the average 1990 exchange rate of ¥145 to the dollar). Our calculation shows an implied nontariff barrier on milled rice of 737 percent in 1989 (table 1.1).

For wheat, an annual import quota is set by the Ministry of Agriculture, Forestry, and Fisheries (MAFF). However, unlike rice, Japan imports significant amounts of wheat; in 1990, for example, only 16 percent of Japan's wheat consumption was domestically produced. The prices paid by the Government Food Agency to domestic wheat producers are much higher than the agency's selling price to the public. The agency finances the difference largely by selling imported wheat at prices significantly above purchase cost. The OECD estimated the subsidy to wheat producers in 1990 at ¥155 billion ($1.1 billion). Our calculations show an implied nontariff barrier of 478 percent for wheat in 1989 (table 1.1).

There are no quantitative restraints on raw sugar imports. However, tariff rates on imported sugar averaged 46 percent in 1991–92, one of the highest rates in Japan's tariff schedule. Moreover, the domestic sugar price is isolated from the world price by a stabilization fund administered by the Japan Raw Silk and Sugar Stabilization Corporation, which holds monopoly power over sugar from both domestic and foreign sources. The domestic price of imported raw sugar is set at a target level. The corporation then pays subsidies to millers, processors, and growers to promote the use of domestic sugar over imported raw sugar. The subsidies are financed both by general government revenues and by levies on imported raw sugar.

The subsidy system for raw sugar production reduces the domestic shipment price, and thus the unit value differential in 1989 was actually negative (table A.3). As a result, raw sugar was not included in our list

---

1. Prior to 1993, extremely limited amounts of rice could be imported for special purposes.

of highly protected products. This is a product category where protection for domestic activity is high but is not captured by our approach. The same omission could occur in other, unidentified product categories.

Unit value differentials in canned and bottled vegetables reflect government policy, which is similar in spirit but applied with less force than the raw sugar policy. Fourteen major vegetables (including cabbages, onions, tomatoes, carrots, and potatoes) are subject to a guaranteed price system administered by the Vegetable Supply Stabilization Fund. The stabilization scheme is funded by three sources: the central government, prefectural governments, and growers. A tariff escalation schedule raises rates on processed vegetables to a range of 7 to 28 percent, against 5 to 10 percent on fresh vegetables. The combination of guaranteed prices, tariffs, and private barriers creates a total barrier of 139 percent for this category (table 1.1).

Soybeans, an economically significant food item in Japan,[2] may be imported duty free. Perhaps as a result, the share of soybean consumption satisfied by domestic producers is only 5 to 7 percent. A deficiency payment scheme is applied to soybean and rapeseed production. In 1990–91, the amount of public financial assistance to soybean and rapeseed producers amounted to ¥19 billion ($134 million; GATT 1992, table V.2). According to our calculations, domestic soybean producers enjoy the nontariff barrier equivalent of 424 percent (table 1.1).

Dairy farming is among the most highly protected large sectors in Japan. The Livestock Industry Promotion Corporation holds monopoly import rights over milk products (butter, skimmed milk powder, condensed whole milk, and skimmed milk), and this power is used to support the domestic price of dairy products. In April 1989, responding to a GATT panel recommendation, Japan abolished its import quotas on processed cheese, frozen yogurt, ice cream, and whipped cream in pressurized containers. Nevertheless, the OECD estimates for assistance given to dairy farmers in Japan showed an overall increase for 1990 and 1991 (GATT 1992, 121). Our calculations show an implied tariff equivalent of 229 percent on dairy products (table 1.1).

The income of dairy farmers also depends on sales of beef as a by-product. Thus, the liberalization of beef imports following the US-Japan Beef Market Access Agreement in 1988 was accompanied by the introduction of a price stabilization scheme for calves as a means of boosting the income of dairy farmers. The scheme enabled calf producers to receive a "guaranteed standard price" regardless of the actual selling price. During the transition period (1987–90), beef import quotas were scheduled to increase by 60,000 tons each year. In accordance with the agreement, quotas on beef imports were terminated in April 1991, but they

---

2. Soybeans are not only used for oil extraction but processed into miso, shoyu, tofu, and natto, which are favorite Japanese foods.

were replaced by much higher tariffs, which increased from 25 percent to 70 percent. It was further agreed that an emergency tariff of 25 percent would be introduced when domestic market disruption occurred. For the broader category, dressed carcasses and poultry, however, the level of implied tariff-equivalent protection is modest by Japanese agricultural standards—just 39 percent (table 1.1).

Import quotas on fresh oranges were terminated in April 1991, and those on orange juice in April 1992. Prior to 1992 these quotas, together with quarantine regulations, created a nontariff barrier for citrus fruits estimated at 114 percent (table 1.1). Since 1992 Japan's fruit growers, including citrus fruit growers, have been mainly protected by high tariffs. Ordinary tariffs and seasonal peak tariffs on oranges are 20 percent and 40 percent, respectively. However, the realized ad valorem tariff was only 14 percent in 1989. Strict quarantine regulations still prohibit citrus imports from many countries.

Tariffs are the main formal trade policy instrument affecting tea and roasted coffee; the nominal rates are 10.0 percent and 13.9 percent, respectively.[3] The realized ad valorem tariff was 11.9 percent in 1989. Nevertheless, private firms seem to be able to keep domestic prices several times the level of import prices, and the calculated nontariff barrier is 707 percent (table 1.1).

Nominal tariff rates on beer and spirits average 22.9 percent. As a result of a GATT panel recommendation in November 1987, the Liquor Tax Law was revised in April 1989 to eliminate tax discrimination against imported spirits, which are generally sold in the luxury market at high prices. The major changes were the abolition of the ad valorem tax on whiskey and brandy and the imposition of tax according to alcoholic content. Yet the calculated nontariff barrier for these products for 1989 was still 88 percent (table 1.1).

A Keidanren report suggested that high prices charged for domestic oats, inclusive of producer subsidies, were a leading reason for high beer prices in Japan (Keidanren 1993; the Keidanren, or Japan Federation of Economic Organizations, is a leading business association in Japan). However, an economic journal, the *Diamond Weekly* (24 July 1993), claimed that the main cause of high domestic prices is the dominance of the Japanese beer market by four major producers (Asahi, Kirin, Suntory, and Sapporo). This seems to be a plausible explanation for the calculated nontariff barrier of 141 percent (table 1.1).

Japan Tobacco holds monopoly purchase rights for leaf tobacco produced in Japan and acts as the sole domestic manufacturer of tobacco products. Responding to US criticism, in late 1989 Japan Tobacco began sourcing at least 50 percent of its leaf inputs from abroad. Prior to this reform, the calculated nontariff barrier for leaf tobacco had been 120

---

3. Import quotas are applied to a blend of coffee that mainly consists of dried milk.

percent (table 1.1). Japan stopped levying the statutory import duty on cigarettes and other tobacco products in 1986, also in response to pressure from the United States. Nevertheless, the calculations here suggest that other regulations or private barriers continue to restrict trade and that the implied tariff equivalent of this protection is 241 percent.

Textiles and Light Industries

Textiles and apparel were Japan's leading exports until the early 1970s. Clothing and knit fabrics experienced a surge of imports in the 1980s. Between 1985 and 1989, imports of these products increased annually at compound rates of 20 percent and 25 percent (table 1.1). By 1990 Japan had become a big net importer of textile and apparel products.

Unlike other industrialized countries, Japan has not yet resorted to import restrictions under the Multi-Fiber Arrangement (MFA). But Japan has restricted Korean exports through a "voluntary export restraint" arrangement; so far it is resisting industry pressure to take action against China under the MFA (MITI 1994). In the past, Japan has tried to rationalize its capital stock and upgrade its product line by providing assistance to troubled textile firms. The Textile Industry Structural Improvement Program (Sen-i Sangyo Kozo Kaizen Sochi) coupled with concessional loans to small and medium-sized firms were the core policy instruments.

Unit value differentials for clothing were already large in 1985, around 300 percent on average, and the figure was particularly high for women's wear. Imports grew rapidly in the late 1980s. For example, imports of women's wear expanded at an annual compound rate of 36 percent between 1985 and 1989.[4] Yet the unit value differentials for clothing remained about the same between 1985 and 1989, still averaging 292 percent in 1989. Why did the unit value differential (and, by implication, the nontariff barrier) remain so high? The reason may be that the domestic apparel industry upgraded its products and surrendered the low-priced apparel market to imports. During the period from 1985 to 1989 the share of Japan's imports of women's wear from China rose from 28 to 34 percent while imports from the European Community dropped from 26 to 22 percent. At least anecdotally, it appears that the relative importance of low-priced imports may have increased (Ide 1990). If so, the continuing large unit value differentials could simply reflect a growing disparity between the type and quality of Japanese apparel and the type and quality of imported apparel, rather than a continuing high level of nontariff barriers.

Starting in 1987 Japan experienced large increases in imports of knit

---

4. This figure is based on detailed data not shown in table 1.1 (see Ide 1990).

products from Korea. Japanese knitwear producers pressured the government to invoke import restrictions under the MFA. In response, in February 1989 Korea placed a voluntary export restraint (VER) on knit exports to Japan. With the VER restraining Korean exports, Chinese knitwear makers increased their share of the Japanese market, at even lower prices. Accordingly, it is difficult to say that the Korean VER pushed up import prices of knit products. In fact, in 1989 knit fabrics showed a zero nontariff barrier rate. The average applied tariff rate in this sector is 8.1 percent, however (table 1.1).

Japan's plywood firms mainly process imported logs. The magnitude of tariff escalation by stage of processing has been reduced since the Tokyo Round. Nevertheless, Japanese tariffs on plywood range from 3.5 to 15 percent, while raw logs are imported tariff free. The implied nontariff barrier rate on plywood is even higher, at 19 percent (table 1.1).

Japan's pulp and paper industry suffers from overcapacity, reflecting the twin effects of a slump in market demand and excessive investment in new factories. The US-Japan five-year agreement (signed in April 1992) was aimed at increasing foreign access to the paper and paperboard markets. The Japan Fair Trade Commission is now looking into impediments emphasized by the US Trade Representative: the absence of written purchase orders for many transactions among Japanese firms (which allows nontransparent contracting practices to flourish) and the custom of making posttransaction price adjustments (which gives Japanese firms a second bite at competing for orders). The impact of such practices is reflected in the implied nontariff rate of 19 percent (table 1.1).

In terms of formal tariff barriers, leather footwear is the most heavily protected category of manufactured goods in Japan. A tariff-quota system is used to restrict imports. Tariffs on imported footwear within the quota are either 21.6 percent, 27 percent, or 30 percent. Above-quota tariff rates are 60 percent or ¥4,800 per pair ($34.80 at the average 1989 exchange rate), whichever is higher. However, the realized tariff rate on footwear is much lower, only 6.4 percent, and the total implied protection is just 14 percent, comparatively low for a protected Japanese industry (table 1.1).

Metal Products

The average unit value differential for the metal products group, although high, was the smallest for the five commodity groups listed in table 1.1, averaging 60 percent. Moreover, tariffs play little role in this sector. Nominal ad valorem tariffs in 1989 were 6.3 percent for aluminum, 5.5 percent for lead, 5.3 percent for copper, 4.5 percent for zinc, and 1.1 percent for tin (realized rates were often lower; see table 1.1). Nearly all the protection for metal products apparently reflects private barriers to the Japanese market.

Sheet glass illustrates the problem. Japan's sheet glass market is supplied primarily by three producers: Asahi Glass, Nippon Sheet Glass, and Central Glass. Not surprisingly, the implied nontariff barrier in 1989 was 62 percent (table 1.1). The US-Japan Structural Impediments Initiative (SII) took up the claim by a US flat glass maker that the domestic distribution network controlled by the three Japanese producers was being used to impede market access. The issue was again taken up in the Global Partnership Action Plan (1992). The Japanese government agreed to facilitate foreign exports to Japan with an import expansion program. The Ministry of Construction is helping foreign firms to meet the standards applied to glass used in Japanese construction. As a follow-up exercise, the Japan Fair Trade Commission (JFTC) surveyed competitive conditions in the Japanese glass market. At the end of 1993, the JFTC reported that it had found no violations of Japan's Anti-Monopoly Law, but it encouraged the three glass producers to terminate a system of sales targets and rebates for distributors that may have had a negative effect on imports (*International Trade Reporter*, 5 January 1994, 10).

Chemical Products

The Japanese petroleum industry is subject to the Petroleum Business Law, whose provisions reflect the importance of energy in a country where natural resources are extremely scarce. This law enables MITI to control imports of petroleum products, including gasoline.

High prices of energy and petroleum products have helped to limit energy consumption in Japan. In 1990 total energy consumption per capita was 2,412 kilograms of oil equivalent in Japan, compared with 5,465 kilograms of oil equivalent in the United States (OECD 1989–90). Although low Japanese energy consumption inflicts less damage on the environment, the high prices of natural gas and petroleum-related products, for example naphtha, exert a dampening effect on downstream industries such as nitric fertilizer production.

The Japanese chemical industry, including chemical fertilizer manufacturing, has experienced excess capacity since the mid-1970s. For a while, adjustment was carried out under the Law on Temporary Measures for Facilitating Industrial Structural Adjustment. This law expired in 1991. Nevertheless, domestic prices of chemical products such as soda ash, caustic soda, and methane derivatives remain substantially higher than the prices of comparable imports. Implied nontariff barriers for these products in 1989 were 149 percent, 219 percent, and 191 percent, respectively (table 1.1).

Although the Poisonous and Deleterious Substance Control Law and the Pharmaceutical Affairs Law are not aimed directly at limiting imports of cosmetics and pharmaceuticals, they have a restrictive effect.

For example, the importation or manufacture of all pharmaceuticals that fall under the Pharmaceutical Affairs Law must be licensed. Approval for a license depends on whether the drug satisfies the standards set by the Japanese Pharmacopoeia. Moreover, only firms resident in Japan are permitted to hold an import license. The nontariff barrier for pharmaceuticals is just 5 percent.

The nontariff barrier rate for cosmetics and toilet preparations is estimated at 660 percent, the third highest among the products under study (table 1.1). Cosmetics that contain ingredients not previously approved must first be evaluated on the basis of test data. The Keidanren (1993) has recommended a simplification of this and other import procedures. For example, the Keidanren suggests that a small amount of imports for sample use could be permitted without prior certification.[5] The Keidanren also argues for increased transparency in implementing the Pharmaceutical Affairs Law.

Machinery

In recent years, high-technology industries, including machinery, have attracted attention in the controversial debate over strategic trade. Analysts such as Laura Tyson (1992) argue that, in high-technology industries, public policy rather than natural endowments can create comparative advantage. Moreover, many countries see these industries as vital to their interests because they are important to national security, because they generate large spillover benefits, and because they create high-skill, high-wage jobs. Using these arguments, Tyson and other US commentators have urged a "cautious activist" approach to achieve lower Japanese barriers in high-technology industries. Many Europeans voice similar views. These arguments seemed to have been influential in guiding US trade policy toward Japan, particularly in the first two years of the Clinton administration.

Our analysis of unit value differentials did not uncover high implied nontariff barriers across a wide spectrum of high-technology product categories. However, we did find evidence of high nontariff barriers on some types of machinery. Tariffs in the machinery categories listed in table 1.1 are nearly zero, but implied nontariff barriers average 140 percent (see table 1.1). US trade negotiators argue that discriminatory government procurement dampens sales of foreign-made computers, while technical standards may inhibit imports of telecommunications and medical equipment (USTR, *National Trade Estimate Report on Foreign Trade Barriers*, 1994; see also Bergsten and Noland 1993, chapter 4).

---

5. At present, under the Pharmaceutical Affairs Law, only 36 items may be imported without prior certification.

An important qualification to this finding must be stressed. Large unit value differentials in the case of radio and television sets mainly reflect differences in quality between Japanese and foreign products. This phenomenon may have been accentuated by yen appreciation over the past 10 years. As the yen has risen in value, Japanese multinationals have begun to produce low-quality items offshore in order to import those goods back to Japan, a practice known as "reverse importing" (Urata 1993). For example, one electronic firm was reported to plan monthly imports of 10,000 basic videocassette players (with no capability for recording) from Malaysia (Japan External Trade Organization 1993). At the same time, VCRs equipped with cameras, which are usually priced more than twice as high as these simple machines, are primarily produced in Japan.

Such examples suggest that unit value differences between domestic and imported products in the consumer electronics category mainly reflect differences in quality or technological sophistication. However, the unit value differentials for other machinery products, such as chemical machinery, electric computing equipment, communications equipment, and medical instruments, cannot be so easily dismissed. In these sectors, US and German producers are competitive in a number of product lines, including at the high end of product quality and sophistication, so that one would not expect to find systematically higher Japanese prices simply because of quality differences. Excluding the radio and television category, where quality differences are known to exist, the average tariff equivalent of implied protection in the other machinery categories is still around 100 percent.

3

The Impact of Japanese Protection

Trade barriers penalize Japanese households and industrial purchasers by restricting demand and raising prices, but they also enable domestic farms and firms to maintain higher output and price levels. In addition, nontariff protection creates "quota rents"—artificial scarcity premiums—that are captured by importers and distributors at the expense of society at large.

The impact of protection can be calculated by comparing the observed situation in 1989, given the existing regime of protection and the observed unit value differentials, with the results from a simulation in which there is no protection and unit value differentials are assumed to be zero. A computable partial equilibrium methodology is used to carry out this simulation. The model is based on Hufbauer and Elliott (1994) and is explained in detail in appendix C. The model makes several assumptions.

First, imported and domestic products are assumed not to be identical in their characteristics, and therefore not perfect substitutes.

Second, all markets—both those for imported and those for domestic products—are assumed to be perfectly competitive, with the result that no firms exercise market power. In reality, however, many domestic markets do exhibit monopolistic tendencies, and an unmeasured side benefit of removing protection is to make these markets more competitive.

Third, it is assumed that all foreign supply elasticities are infinite. Hence the presence or absence of Japanese protection is assumed to have no effect on world prices, and thus no effect on the Japanese terms of trade.

Fourth, the model is a partial equilibrium model in the following sense: it evaluates the impact of protection only on the product under consideration and ignores the impact on upstream or downstream products. This simplifying assumption misses part of the picture if removing protection on a certain product significantly affects consumption and production elsewhere in the economic chain.

Fifth, only the static effects of removing protection are examined in the simulation. The possible dynamic effects are not taken into account. One important dynamic impact of opening markets is improved efficiency within Japan. To meet more intense competition from abroad, domestic producers usually attempt to reduce costs by upgrading their management and improving their technical efficiency; sometimes they launch new products as well. These dynamic reactions can substantially enhance the static benefits derived from liberalization.

The second and fifth assumptions of the Hufbauer-Elliott model are particularly important. Together they ensure that the model used will understate the gains from liberalization of any given trade barrier. Richardson (1989) has shown that, when the reduction of import barriers undermines domestic monopolies, oligopolies, and cartels, freer trade yields significant additional benefits. Various authors—for example, Caves and Krepps (1993), Edwards (1993), Romer (1994), and Hufbauer and Schott (1994)—have shown that trade liberalization boosts efficiency in protected industries and raises GDP growth rates. Thus, even though the problem of quality and type differentials may cause our calculations to overstate the level of Japanese protection in particular sectors, other considerations indicate that we may have understated the adverse impact that protection imposes on the Japanese economy.

Elasticity Parameters

Various elasticity parameters are necessary to perform the simulation exercises. Specifically, we needed to estimate the own-price elasticity of demand for the domestic product (E_{dd}), the own-price elasticity of demand for the imported product (E_{mm}), the cross-price elasticity of demand for the domestic product with respect to the price of the imported product (E_{dm}), the cross-price elasticity of demand for the imported product with respect to the price of the domestic product (E_{md}), and the own-price elasticity of supply for the domestic product (E_s). In addition, the average employment-output ratio for 1985, taken from the Japanese input-output table (Management and Coordination Agency 1989), is used to calculate the effect of protection on employment. Our estimates for the various demand and supply elasticities, and the employment-output ratio, appear in table 3.1.

To estimate the demand elasticities, we began by computing regression estimates for the parameters of demand equations based on the "almost ideal demand system" developed in Deaton and Muellbauer

(1980).[1] We then adjusted the computed elasticities, using various econometric techniques, if they contradicted the principles of microeconomic theory, or if they had unreasonable magnitudes. For instance, if a demand elasticity or cross-elasticity failed to have the expected sign, or appeared to have an extreme value, the elasticity was adjusted. Starting with the adjusted demand elasticities, we then derived supply elasticities according to the relationships outlined in appendix B.

Results of the Simulation

The results of the simulation exercise are summarized in tables 3.2, 3.3, and 3.4.[2] They show that, in the aggregate, the total quantity of imports of the products under study might double if the observed unit value differentials were eliminated. In contrast, using the same partial equilibrium model but a different methodology for estimating tariff equivalents of nontariff barriers, Hufbauer and Elliott (1994) found that, in 1990, US imports of highly protected goods would have increased by about 30 percent. (Additional comparisons with US experience, all of which are taken from Hufbauer and Elliott 1994 and apply to the year 1990, are cited in the paragraphs that follow.) In Japan, domestic output of highly protected products would decline by only 9 percent with the elimination of unit value differentials. As a result of the increase in imports and the decrease in production, the Japanese import penetration ratio in real terms (i.e., measured in prices prior to the elimination of the differentials) for highly protected industries would on average increase from 10 to 23 percent.

In terms of standard welfare measures, the elimination of unit value differentials for highly protected industries would increase consumer surplus by ¥15 trillion (approximately $110 billion at the 1989 average market exchange rate of ¥138 to the dollar). These gains include those realized by industrial users of protected commodities as product inputs. The comparable US figure for highly protected industries is $32 billion. The Japanese figure amounts to 25 percent of the value of consumption of the goods under study (table 3.3), whereas the US ratio is only 12 percent.

An increase in Japanese consumer surplus of ¥15 trillion would roughly equal 3.8 percent of Japanese GDP and 6.6 percent of total private consumption. On a per capita basis, consumers would be better off by

---

1. For information on the methods used to estimate demand elasticities, the interested reader should consult Hiroki Kawai (see page iv).

2. The tables present the results for all 47 sectors that had unit value differentials greater than 5 percent in 1989. The results excluding sectors that exhibited instability in the sensitivity analysis are discussed below.

Table 3.1 Parameters used in the partial computable equilibrium model

Sector and product category	Demand elasticities				Domestic supply elasticity (E_s)	Labor-output ratio[a] (L/Qd)
	E_{dd}	E_{dm}	E_{mm}	E_{md}		
Food and beverages						
Wheat	-0.203	0.203	-0.270	0.270	0.500	0.201
Soybeans	-0.180	0.180	-0.196	0.196	0.500	0.468
Citrus fruits	-0.148	0.148	-0.297	0.297	0.349	0.376
Oilseeds other than soybeans	-0.479	0.479	-0.487	0.487	0.500	0.042
Leaf tobacco	-0.521	0.521	-1.890	1.890	1.602	0.439
Dressed carcasses (beef, pork, etc.) and poultry	-0.210	0.210	-0.953	0.953	0.375	0.020
Processed meat products	-0.169	0.169	-0.731	0.731	0.720	0.028
Dairy products	-0.104	0.104	-0.333	0.333	1.604	0.023
Milled rice	-0.101	0.101	-0.936	0.936	0.049	0.002
Bread	-0.128	0.128	-0.874	0.874	0.268	0.061
Confectionery goods	-0.160	0.160	-1.043	1.043	0.042	0.063
Canned or bottled vegetables and fruits	-1.086	1.086	-2.257	2.257	0.500	0.045
Beer	-0.161	0.161	-0.795	0.795	0.986	0.006
Whiskey and brandy	-0.396	0.396	-0.689	0.689	0.500	0.008
Tea and roasted coffee	-0.123	0.123	-0.801	0.801	0.470	0.030
Sparkling and still beverages	-0.120	0.120	-2.885	2.885	1.202	0.021
Tobacco products	-0.274	0.274	-2.674	2.674	0.537	0.009
Textiles and light industries						
Cotton yarn	-0.307	0.307	-0.502	0.502	0.247	0.088
Knit fabrics	-0.295	0.295	-1.750	1.750	0.257	0.102
Clothing	-0.119	0.119	-0.637	0.637	0.726	0.078
Plywood	-0.127	0.127	-1.244	1.244	0.500	0.055
Paper	-0.100	0.100	-0.725	0.725	0.113	0.022
Leather footwear	-0.284	0.284	-2.693	2.693	1.884	0.061

	E_{dd}	E_{dm}	E_{mm}	E_{md}	E_s	Employees[a]
Metal products						
Copper ore	-0.114	0.114	-0.184	0.184	0.500	0.043
Sheet glass	-1.060	1.060	-1.504	1.504	0.500	0.029
Clay refractories	-0.151	0.151	-2.784	2.784	0.752	0.040
Ferroalloys	-0.364	0.364	-0.638	0.638	0.500	0.019
Lead (incl. regenerated)	-0.495	0.495	-0.572	0.572	0.063	0.031
Regenerated aluminum	-0.141	0.141	-0.833	0.833	0.091	0.010
Other nonferrous metals	-1.285	1.285	-2.860	2.860	0.500	0.024
Chemical products						
Natural gas	-0.245	0.245	-0.305	0.305	0.500	0.015
Nitric fertilizers	-0.136	0.136	-1.051	1.051	0.435	0.024
Soda ash	-0.167	0.167	-0.839	0.839	0.763	0.021
Caustic soda	-0.147	0.147	-0.870	0.870	0.325	0.018
Titanium oxide	-0.440	0.440	-2.327	2.327	1.224	0.025
Methane derivatives	-0.176	0.176	-1.025	1.025	0.408	0.019
Industrial oil and fat	-0.484	0.484	-2.355	2.355	0.406	0.045
Polyethylene	-0.147	0.147	-0.870	0.870	0.271	0.015
Pharmaceuticals	-0.128	0.128	-1.048	1.048	0.249	0.031
Cosmetics, toilet preparations	-0.137	0.137	-1.465	1.465	1.740	0.012
Gasoline	-0.137	0.137	-0.924	0.924	0.649	0.002
Machinery						
Chemical machinery	-0.160	0.160	-1.506	1.506	0.558	0.040
Radio and television sets	-0.266	0.266	-1.972	1.972	0.551	0.021
Electric computing equipment	-0.121	0.121	-0.530	0.530	1.108	0.041
Communication equipment	-0.111	0.111	-1.243	1.243	1.206	0.081
Semiconductor devices	-0.254	0.254	-2.751	2.751	0.777	0.051
Medical instruments	-0.222	0.222	-1.246	1.246	0.603	0.061

E_{dd} = own-price elasticity of demand for domestic goods; E_{dm} = cross-price elasticity of demand for domestic goods with respect to imported goods; E_{mm} = own-price elasticity of demand for imported goods; E_{md} = cross-price elasticity of demand for imported goods with respect to domestic goods; E_s = own-price elasticity of supply for domestic producers.

a. Number of employees per million yen of output at 1989 prices.

Sources: Authors' estimates based on Japanese input-output tables (Management and Coordination Agency 1989, and MITI, various years). Interested readers may contact Hiroki Kawai (see p. iv) for an explanation of statistical methods used to estimate these parameters.

Table 3.2 Calculated effects of removing protection on imports and domestic production, 1989[a]

Sector and product category	Import price (index)[b]	Import quantity (billions of 1989 yen)	Change in import quantity (percentages)	Domestic price (index)[b]	Domestic production quantity (billions of 1989 yen)	Change in domestic production quantity (percentages)	Import penetration (percentages)[c] Real	Import penetration (percentages)[c] Nominal
Food and beverages	**0.373**	**4,928**	**146.3**	**0.670**	**17,000**	**-12.0**	**22.5**	**13.9**
Wheat	0.173	229	40.0	0.602	125	-22.4	64.6	34.4
Soybeans	0.191	235	27.0	0.645	48	-19.7	82.9	59.0
Citrus fruits	0.438	94	18.8	0.782	267	-8.2	26.0	16.5
Oilseeds other than soybeans	0.137	136	63.9	0.378	0	-38.5	99.7	99.2
Leaf tobacco	0.455	9	207.0	0.824	100	-26.6	8.6	4.9
Dressed carcasses (beef, pork, etc.) and poultry	0.722	759	22.1	0.889	1,848	-4.3	29.1	25.0
Processed meat products	0.455	49	59.4	0.861	750	-10.2	6.1	3.3
Dairy products	0.304	120	45.0	0.930	430	-10.9	21.9	8.4
Milled rice	0.119	4	91.9	0.240	2,833	-6.8	0.1	0.1
Bread	0.224	3	142.2	0.616	885	-12.2	0.3	0.1
Confectionery goods	0.322	74	27.7	0.407	1,181	-3.7	5.9	4.7
Canned or bottled vegetables and fruits	0.418	172	86.0	0.550	282	-25.8	37.9	31.7
Beer	0.412	44	83.4	0.883	2,029	-11.6	2.1	1.0
Whiskey and brandy	0.515	375	29.0	0.746	405	-13.6	48.1	39.0
Tea and roasted coffee	0.122	73	280.0	0.647	488	-18.5	13.0	2.7
Sparkling and still beverages	0.337	467	1,637.5	0.906	2,115	-11.2	18.1	7.6
Tobacco products	0.293	2,086	778.4	0.661	3,214	-19.9	39.4	22.4
Textiles and light industries	**0.512**	**2,095**	**53.6**	**0.906**	**4,737**	**-4.9**	**30.7**	**20.0**
Cotton yarn	0.716	90	7.7	0.831	322	-4.5	21.9	19.5
Knit fabrics	0.925	481	6.6	0.959	1,243	-1.1	27.9	27.2
Clothing	0.255	1,197	111.2	0.824	1,174	-13.1	50.5	24.0
Plywood	0.765	207	30.4	0.947	969	-2.7	17.6	14.7
Paper	0.819	79	8.0	0.910	865	-1.1	8.4	7.6
Leather footwear	0.879	41	35.3	0.983	165	-3.1	20.1	18.4
Metal products	**0.711**	**1,419**	**18.6**	**0.829**	**1,942**	**-8.3**	**42.2**	**38.5**
Copper ore	0.386	301	15.4	0.838	3	-8.5	99.1	98.0
Sheet glass	0.613	47	26.6	0.717	570	-15.3	7.6	6.6
Clay refractories	0.357	98	991.7	0.842	339	-12.1	22.4	10.9

Ferroalloys	0.822	191	7.5	0.921	229	−4.0	45.4	42.7
Lead (incl. regenerated)	0.811	9	1.4	0.830	62	−1.2	12.5	12.3
Regenerated aluminum	0.795	188	7.8	0.870	544	−1.3	25.6	24.0
Other nonferrous metals	0.881	587	10.7	0.913	196	−4.5	75.0	74.3
Chemical products	**0.428**	**2,429**	**79.2**	**0.902**	**11,288**	**−6.6**	**17.7**	**9.3**
Natural gas	0.469	899	16.8	0.779	69	−11.7	92.8	88.6
Nitric fertilizers	0.541	10	63.5	0.864	37	−6.2	20.9	14.2
Soda ash	0.402	12	87.1	0.849	41	−11.7	22.9	12.3
Caustic soda	0.309	3	102.1	0.694	170	−11.2	1.7	0.8
Titanium oxide	0.715	35	77.5	0.915	95	−10.3	26.8	22.2
Methane derivates	0.341	81	116.0	0.724	126	−12.4	39.2	23.3
Industrial oil and fat	0.691	17	48.7	0.818	68	−7.8	19.6	17.0
Polyethylene	0.751	38	17.5	0.904	1,319	−2.7	2.8	2.3
Pharmaceuticals	0.922	418	5.8	0.973	5,513	−0.7	7.0	6.7
Cosmetics, toilet preparations	0.131	863	1,476.3	0.862	647	−22.7	57.2	16.9
Gasoline	0.304	53	148.0	0.812	3,201	−12.6	1.6	0.6
Machinery	**0.448**	**3,585**	**181.4**	**0.888**	**13,958**	**−10.0**	**20.4**	**11.5**
Chemical machinery	0.621	104	74.7	0.899	1,077	−5.8	8.8	6.2
Radio and television sets	0.141	595	1,249.9	0.529	720	−29.6	45.2	18.1
Electric computing equipment	0.569	751	30.9	0.946	6,003	−6.0	11.1	7.0
Communication equipment	0.297	319	298.0	0.903	2407	−11.6	11.7	4.2
Semiconductor devices	0.484	1,612	349.8	0.836	3,059	−13.0	34.5	23.4
Medical instruments	0.754	205	29.3	0.927	692	−4.5	22.9	19.4
Total for listed products	**0.454**	**14,457**	**101.0**	**0.815**	**48,926**	**−9.4**	**22.8**	**14.1**

a. See appendix C for the computable partial equilibrium model used to calculate these results. Figures for sectors and for total listed products are value-weighted averages of the product categories they contain, using import values or domestic production values, as appropriate.

b. Units are defined for each product so that the landed import price, including the effects of protection, and the domestic ex-farm or ex-factory price per unit is 1.000 before liberalization. The import price per unit after liberalization is derived from the preliberalization price in index form by adjusting for the tariff equivalent, $t + nt$, of tariff and nontariff barriers, using the following formula: $Pm = 1.000/(1 + t + nt)$. Values for $(t + nt)$ are found by dividing the unit value differences in table 1 by 100.0. The domestic price declines in response to the fall in the import price.

c. The figure for real import penetration is calculated as: $Qm/(Qd + Qm)$. The figure for nominal import penetration, taking into account import and domestic prices after the removal of protection, is: $PmQm/(PdQd + PmQm)$. In these definitions, Qm, Qd, Pm, and Pd, respectively, represent import quantity, domestic production quantity, import price, and domestic ex-farm or ex-factory price.

Sources: Data on imports from Japan Tariff Association (1990). All other data are from the Japanese input-output tables (Management and Coordination Agency 1989, and MITI, various years).

Table 3.3 Calculated welfare effects of removing protection, 1989[a] (billions of 1989 yen unless noted otherwise)

Sector and product category	Consumer surplus gain (A + B + C + D)	Producer surplus loss (A)	Tariff revenue decline (B)	Quota rents eliminated (C)	Efficiency gain (D)	Consumer surplus ratio (percentages)
Food and beverages	**8,058.5**	**5,963.0**	**149.8**	**953.5**	**992.1**	**37.8**
Wheat	219.4	57.0	0.0	135.2	27.1	67.5
Soybeans	189.2	19.3	0.0	149.7	20.2	77.1
Citrus fruits	109.3	60.7	9.8	34.6	4.2	29.6
Oilseeds other than soybeans	94.5	0.3	0.0	71.4	22.8	113.4
Leaf tobacco	24.2	20.8	0.0	1.7	1.7	17.3
Dressed carcasses (beef, pork, etc.) and poultry	401.2	208.9	77.1	96.1	19.1	15.7
Processed meat products	132.1	110.4	4.7	12.0	5.0	15.3
Dairy products	102.4	31.8	12.4	45.3	13.0	18.1
Milled rice	2,235.6	2,233.0	0.0	1.8	0.8	73.5
Bread	364.0	363.0	0.1	0.8	0.6	36.1
Confectionery goods	758.8	714.0	9.2	30.2	5.5	59.1
Canned or bottled vegetables and fruits	225.6	148.6	14.1	39.7	23.2	47.8
Beer	273.1	253.2	0.4	13.7	5.9	11.8
Whiskey and brandy	272.3	111.1	16.1	124.7	20.4	35.9
Tea and roasted coffee	232.2	192.0	2.0	14.7	23.5	37.6
Sparkling and still beverages	376.1	212.4	3.9	13.9	145.9	15.6
Tobacco products	2,047.7	1,226.6	0.0	167.8	653.2	48.2
Textiles and light industries	**1,239.1**	**461.1**	**112.0**	**422.2**	**243.8**	**19.5**
Cotton yarn	80.4	55.7	4.2	19.6	0.9	19.1
Knit fabrics	85.9	50.9	33.8	0.0	1.1	5.0
Clothing	878.9	221.6	53.3	369.1	234.9	45.8
Plywood	94.8	51.9	16.4	20.8	5.7	8.2
Foreign paper and Japanese paper	92.0	78.2	2.3	10.9	0.5	9.7
Leather footwear	7.1	2.8	1.8	1.9	0.7	3.6

Metal products	712.3	351.3	10.6	301.5	48.8	21.5
Copper ore	172.8	0.5	0.0	160.1	12.3	65.6
Sheet glass	192.0	175.8	0.5	13.8	1.9	27.0
Clay refractories	91.7	57.3	0.1	5.7	28.6	23.2
Ferroalloys	51.3	18.5	6.1	25.5	1.2	12.3
Lead (incl. regenerated)	12.2	10.5	0.3	1.4	0.0	17.2
Regenerated aluminum	108.5	71.3	1.4	34.3	1.4	15.0
Other nonferrous metals	83.9	17.5	2.3	60.8	3.4	11.3
Chemical products	2,139.0	1,168.3	18.6	533.5	418.5	15.9
Natural gas	459.7	16.3	0.0	409.1	34.4	54.2
Nitric fertilizers	8.9	5.3	0.0	2.8	0.9	19.4
Soda ash	12.3	6.6	0.0	3.9	1.7	23.0
Caustic soda	57.0	55.4	0.1	1.0	0.5	29.5
Titanium oxide	16.3	8.6	0.8	4.8	2.2	12.9
Methane derivatives	76.6	37.4	0.9	24.0	14.4	42.1
Industrial oil and fat	17.2	12.9	0.1	3.4	0.8	20.2
Polyethylene	137.2	128.5	1.7	6.3	0.7	9.9
Pharmaceuticals	182.9	151.0	12.9	18.0	0.9	3.1
Cosmetics, toilet preparations	500.6	102.1	1.1	46.4	351.0	56.2
Gasoline	670.3	644.3	1.1	13.8	11.1	18.2
Machinery	2,979.2	1,695.5	3.5	584.2	696.0	17.7
Chemical machinery	142.7	111.7	0.0	22.5	8.4	11.9
Radio and television sets	684.0	409.8	0.0	37.8	236.4	64.2
Electric computing equipment	620.0	334.5	0.0	247.2	38.3	8.9
Communication equipment	389.3	249.3	0.0	56.2	83.8	13.9
Semiconductor devices	1,046.6	538.3	0.1	184.8	323.4	27.1
Medical instruments	96.6	51.9	3.3	35.7	5.7	10.9
Total for listed products	**15,128.0**	**9,639.3**	**294.5**	**2,795.0**	**2,399.1**	**24.7**

a. See appendix C for the methodology used to calculate consumer surplus, producer surplus, tariff revenue, quota rents, and efficiency gains. Quota rents are computed as the value equivalent of nontariff barriers (i.e., the difference, expressed in value terms between unit value differentials and realized ad valorem tariffs). The consumer surplus ratio is defined as the consumer surplus gain divided by the value of imports plus domestic production before liberalization (from table 1.1).

Sources: Authors' estimates based on Japanese input-output tables (Management and Coordination Agency 1989, and MITI, various years).

Table 3.4 Calculated employment effects of removing protection, 1989

Sector and product category	Employment before liberalization (thousands of workers)[a]	Change in employment[b]		Cost of preserving a job (millions of yen)	
		Thousands of workers	Percentages	Consumer cost[c]	Efficiency cost[d]
Food and beverages	**510.1**	**-76.6**	**-15.0**	**105.1**	**12.9**
Wheat	25.2	-7.3	-22.4	30.1	3.7
Soybeans	22.6	-5.5	-19.7	34.1	3.6
Citrus fruits	100.2	-9.0	-8.2	12.2	0.5
Oilseeds other than soybeans	negl.	negl.	-38.5	9,750.8	2,353.8
Leaf tobacco	43.9	-15.9	-26.6	1.5	0.1
Dressed carcasses (beef, pork, etc.) and poultry	37.4	-1.7	-4.3	239.2	11.4
Processed meat products	21.3	-2.4	-10.2	54.4	2.0
Dairy products	9.7	-1.2	-10.9	85.9	10.9
Milled rice	5.0	-0.4	-6.8	6,148.0	2.3
Bread	53.6	-7.4	-12.2	49.0	0.1
Confectionery goods	74.0	-2.8	-3.7	267.8	1.9
Canned or bottled vegetables and fruits	12.7	-4.4	-25.8	51.1	5.2
Beer	12.2	-1.6	-11.6	171.5	3.7
Whiskey and brandy	3.3	-0.5	-13.6	520.7	39.1
Tea and roasted coffee	14.7	-3.3	-18.5	69.6	7.0
Sparkling and still beverages	44.1	-5.6	-11.2	67.4	26.1
Tobacco products	30.3	-7.6	-19.9	270.9	86.4
Textiles and light industries	**328.5**	**-18.5**	**-5.6**	**67.1**	**13.2**
Cotton yarn	28.4	-1.3	-4.5	60.7	0.7
Knit fabrics	126.6	-1.4	-1.1	63.0	0.8
Clothing	91.8	-13.8	-13.1	63.7	17.0
Plywood	52.9	-1.5	-2.7	65.1	3.9
Foreign paper and Japanese paper	18.8	-0.2	-1.1	457.5	2.6
Leather footwear	10.0	-0.3	-3.1	22.2	2.0
Metal products	**46.3**	**-5.3**	**-11.6**	**133.2**	**9.1**
Copper ore	0.1	negl.	-8.5	15,727.5	1,118.5
Sheet glass	16.4	-3.0	-15.3	64.6	0.6

Product				
Clay refractories	13.5	−1.9	−12.1	15.3
Ferroalloys	4.4	−0.2	−4.0	6.4
Lead (incl. regenerated)	1.9	negl.	−1.2	0.5
Regenerated aluminum	5.2	−0.06	−1.3	21.1
Other nonferrous metals	4.7	−0.2	−4.5	15.3
Chemical products	**219.9**	**−6.5**	**−3.0**	**64.1**
Natural gas	1.0	−0.1	−11.7	251.0
Nitric fertilizers	0.9	−0.06	−6.2	14.8
Soda ash	0.9	−0.1	−11.7	15.1
Caustic soda	3.0	−0.4	−11.2	1.4
Titanium oxide	2.4	−0.3	−10.3	8.0
Methane derivatives	2.4	−0.3	−12.4	42.7
Industrial oil and fat	3.1	−0.6	−7.8	3.2
Polyethylene	20.0	−1.2	−2.7	1.3
Pharmaceuticals	172.2	−2.3	−0.7	0.8
Cosmetics, toilet preparations	8.0	−0.2	−22.7	149.5
Gasoline	6.1	−0.9	−12.6	12.5
Machinery	**696.4**	**−75.2**	**−10.8**	**9.3**
Chemical machinery	43.1	−2.6	−5.8	3.2
Radio and television sets	14.8	−6.2	−29.6	38.0
Electric computing equipment	245.9	−15.6	−6.0	2.5
Communication equipment	193.9	−25.4	−11.6	3.3
Semiconductor devices	156.5	−23.3	−13.0	13.9
Medical instruments	42.1	−2.0	−4.5	2.9
Total for listed products	**1,801.2**	**−182.2**	**−10.1**	**13.2**

a. Employment as shown in this table consists of production workers and is somewhat smaller than total employment (which includes administrative employees) given in other sources. For all the listed products, total employment is 2,052,300 workers, whereas this table records 1,801,200 workers.

b. Calculated on the basis of the labor-output ratio (table 3.1) and the change in employment (table 3.2).

c. The total consumer cost for each product category reflects higher prices paid by consumers for both domestic and imported goods on account of trade protection. Consumer cost per job is calculated by dividing total consumer cost (table 3.3) by the change in employment (this table).

d. The efficiency cost for each product category reflects the deadweight loss that results from using resources in less productive activities on account of trade protection. Efficiency cost per job is calculated by dividing total efficiency cost (table 3.3) by the change in employment (this table).

Sources: Authors' estimates based on Japanese input–output tables (Management and Coordination Agency 1989, and MITI, various years).

approximately ¥122,000 (about $890 at the average 1989 exchange rate). In contrast, the potential US consumer gains from free trade in highly protected industries would be about 0.6 percent of US GDP and 0.9 percent of US personal consumption. Potential US gains amount to about $130 per capita.

It should be stressed that the cost estimates both for Japan and for the United States do not take into account either the antimonopoly benefits of free trade or the spur that free trade provides to efficiency in the protected industries themselves. If these dynamic gains were counted, they would substantially increase the static magnitudes we have estimated.

The overall effect of protection on the Japanese economy masks wide variations among different sectors. According to OECD estimates (1993), total transfers from Japanese consumers to producers during 1992 for agricultural products alone were estimated at $600 per capita (substantially above the $440 average for all OECD countries).

As an indicator of sectoral effects, it is useful to examine the ratio between the value of consumer surplus obtained from the elimination of unit value differentials and the value of consumption. By this indicator, protection has a very substantial impact on food and beverages (38 percent) and metal products (21 percent). The corresponding ratios for the remaining sectors are between 15 and 19 percent (table 3.3).

Closer examination of the effects of protection at a disaggregated level reveals that certain subsectors are protected to an unusual extent. Interpreting a ratio between consumer surplus and the value of consumption of 30 percent or more as evidence of substantial protection, we find 16 high-impact subsectors. Among these, 10 are in the food and beverage sector (wheat, soybeans, oilseeds, milled rice, bread, confectionery, canned or bottled vegetables and fruits, whiskey and brandy, tea and roasted coffee, and tobacco), 3 are in the chemical products sector (natural gas, methane derivatives, and cosmetics), and 1 each is in the metal products sector (copper ore), the textiles and light industries sector (clothing), and the machinery sector (radio and television sets). However, high ratios for radio and television sets, and for clothing, may reflect not protection but statistical problems resulting from quality differences between the items compared. The results for these two sectors should also be viewed with caution because the unit value differential estimates were not stable in some of the sensitivity tests.

With complete liberalization, Japanese imports would have increased dramatically in 1989 (table 3.2). Total imports in the highly protected industries would have doubled, an increase of ¥7.3 trillion ($53 billion). Since Japan's merchandise imports in 1989 totaled ¥33.8 trillion ($236 billion), an increase of this magnitude would amount to more than 20 percent of base-year imports. The comparable figure for the United States is $16 billion in additional imports, or about 3 percent of base-year imports.

It would be erroneous to suppose that complete liberalization would decrease Japan's trade surplus by anywhere near ¥7.3 trillion. Reallocation of resources within Japan, together with macroeconomic forces, would ensure that, in a liberalization scenario, Japanese exports would increase nearly as much as Japanese imports.

As a consequence of liberalization, the unit values realized by Japanese domestic producers would decline; this would cause a fall in output and a drop in producer surplus. These effects are shown in tables 3.2 and 3.3. The fall in output depends not only on the magnitude of the unit value differential being removed, but also on the sensitivity of the demand for the domestic product with respect to the decline in import prices (the cross-price elasticity) and the response of domestic production with respect to the change in domestic price (the domestic supply elasticity).

Production in certain sectors would decline by more than 20 percent: wheat, oilseeds, leaf tobacco, canned and bottled vegetables and fruits, and cosmetics and toilet preparations. On a sectoral basis, the magnitude of the decline in production is estimated to be high for the protected segments of the food and beverage sector (12 percent). This would be expected because of the significant unit value differentials in this sector. More surprising, production in the protected segments of the machinery sector might decline by 10 percent. This rather large drop can be partly explained by high supply elasticities. This estimate may also exaggerate the actual impact on the machinery sector because quality differences that can cause the observed unit value differentials to overstate the actual degree of protection are particularly severe in this sector.

Producer surplus would decline by ¥9.6 trillion (about $70 billion), equivalent to 18 percent of the value of production at prices prevailing before the elimination of unit value differentials. In contrast, producer surplus in the United States would decline by just 8 percent of the value of production with the elimination of US unit value differentials. More than 60 percent of the decline in Japanese producer surplus would come in the food and beverage sectors, indicating that affected firms would lose significantly from liberalization.

In addition, importers and distributors (mainly Japanese firms but also some foreign firms) would lose quota rents amounting to about ¥2.8 trillion (about $20 billion), equivalent to some 7 percent of total Japanese imports. In contrast, if the United States liberalized, the loss of quota rents would be $7 billion, under 2 percent of total US imports. In both countries the potential loss of quota rents by privileged importers and distributors represents a potential gain to the rest of society.

Japanese employment in the protected industries would fall as a result of liberalization (table 3.4). Our calculations indicate that employment in the industries under study would fall by about 180,000 workers, or 10 percent of the relevant labor force, as a consequence of the total elimination of the measured unit value differentials. The figure for the United States is also about 10 percent. This extent of job loss in Japan amounts to 0.3 percent of overall Japanese employment; for the United States the figure is 0.2 percent. Although these figures seem small, in both countries they would impose substantial adjustment burdens on individual workers, almost certainly requiring some degree of public assistance. However, in both countries the adjustment burden would be significantly eased as other firms created new jobs in more efficient industries, including export production.

The costs to the economy and to consumers of preserving jobs through import protection are quite high. On average in 1989, the Japanese consumer cost per job saved amounted to ¥83 million ($600,000). The figure for the United States was about $170,000. In certain Japanese sectors the consumer costs per job saved were much higher. In chemical products, the figure was nearly ¥330 million ($2.4 million), followed by a figure of ¥133 million ($1 million) for metal products.

Elimination of tariffs would modestly affect the Japanese government. The government would incur a revenue loss of ¥294 billion (about $2 billion), or only 0.5 percent of total government revenue.

The overall efficiency gain from the elimination of unit value differentials may be calculated by subtracting the losses to producers, importers and distributors, and the government from the benefits to consumers. We estimate the net benefit to be ¥2.4 trillion yen (about $17.4 billion), about 0.6 percent of Japanese GDP. The comparable figure for the United States is $4 billion, under 0.1 percent of US GDP. However, in both cases these static figures again represent understated estimates of the cost of trade barriers, because they do not count the potential dynamic gains from liberalization.

Import protection preserves jobs in favored sectors, but at the cost of lower output in the rest of the economy. Counting only static costs, we estimate that the lost economic efficiency of preserving one job for one year costs ¥13 million (about $94,000). Since average annual earnings for a Japanese worker were ¥4.8 million in 1989 (about $34,800), the cost of preserving a job through import protection was roughly 2.7 times greater than the earnings of an average worker. The static efficiency cost for the United States was $54,000, about 1.7 times US average earnings of $31,000 per worker. Evidently, in both countries the provision of public compensation to displaced workers would be a far less costly method of preserving household income.

Adjusting these results to account for the products that had unstable unit value differentials in any of the sensitivity tests—clothing, paper, leather footwear, sheet glass, clay refactories, other nonferrous metals, nitric fertilizers, and radio and television sets—does not significantly change the bottom line. Removing those categories lowers the estimate of consumer surplus only slightly, to ¥13 trillion. An even more conservative estimate, however, might also subtract the more heterogenous categories where quality differences may be a more important factor in explaining some part of the observed unit value differentials. If, in addition to the eight categories above, all product categories in the machinery sector, pharmaceuticals, and cosmetics are ignored, the cost to Japanese consumers of the remaining barriers is still ¥10 trillion, or 2.6 percent of 1989 GNP. Imports in the remaining categories would have increased nearly 50 percent, or ¥3.3 trillion ($24 billion) if barriers were removed, and net national welfare in Japan would have increased by ¥1.1 trillion ($8 billion).

Recalling that the assumptions of the partial equilibrium model used to calculate the welfare effects of protection may lead to understatement of the costs in several ways, a range of ¥10 trillion to ¥13 trillion (roughly $75 billion to $100 billion) seems a reasonable estimate of the costs of protection to Japanese consumers.

Conclusion

Trade protection in Japan is substantial and imposes large costs on Japanese households and industrial purchasers. Measured by unit value differentials between domestic and imported goods, protection imposes a cost of between ¥10 trillion and ¥15 trillion ($75 billion to $110 billion) on Japanese consumers and industrial purchasers, while enriching Japanese producers, importers, and distributors by around ¥9 trillion to ¥12 trillion ($65 billion to $90 billion). The government collects a mere ¥0.3 trillion (under $2 billion) through higher tariffs.

Different types of restrictions are applied to different sectors. Japanese protection is concentrated in agriculture and selected materials (notably nonferrous metals). These same industries are hindered by Japan's poor endowment of natural resources. In other words, protection seems mainly designed to offset Japan's comparative disadvantage in natural resource activities. However, protection also limits Japanese imports of some high-technology products, including some types of machinery.

The bulk of Japanese protection is achieved not through formal tariffs but through nontariff barriers, which exceeded 400 percent for some product categories in 1989. As discussed in chapter 2, some of the formal quotas and other restrictions on food products have been liberalized since 1989. The 20 percent yen appreciation between 1989 and 1993, coupled with flat Japanese wholesale prices, implies that remaining import barriers are even more restrictive today.

Straightforward government intervention restricts imports of food and beverages. As a consequence, food and beverage products are marked by large unit value differentials, averaging 281 percent in 1989. If government protection were removed and these differentials disappeared, consumers' welfare would increase by about 38 percent of the value of consumption, while imports would increase by 146 percent.

The factors that limit imports of metals and chemicals include government policies in the petroleum and pharmaceutical industries that were not principally designed to restrict imports but indirectly have that effect. In addition, restrictive business practices found in sectors such as sheet glass serve to inhibit imports. As a consequence, unit value differentials amount to 60 percent for metals and 129 percent for chemicals. Free trade could increase imports by 19 percent in metals and 79 percent in chemicals. Even calculated conservatively, ignoring the categories with unstable differentials as well as the more heterogeneous cosmetics and pharmaceuticals categories, prices for the remaining metals and chemicals would fall by 53 percent and 164 percent, respectively, and imports in these sectors would increase by 20 percent on average.

There are no explicitly discriminatory government policies in the machinery sector, but government procurement policies and technical standards have been alleged by US firms and trade negotiators to restrict imports of computers, and telecommunications and medical equipment. In global terms, Japan is a highly competitive machinery producer, as its substantial machinery exports show. Nevertheless, certain aspects of Japanese industrial organization may restrict Japanese imports of machinery. The United States has long complained about restrictive practices that limit Japanese imports of communications equipment and computers. Statistical difficulties are severe in this sector. However, if the unit value differentials we have calculated essentially reflect import restrictions rather than quality differences, Japanese restrictions in the six machinery categories considered here might limit imports by as much as ¥2.3 trillion ($17 billion).

For all the highly protected sectors covered in this study, Japanese import restrictions imposed a net cost on Japanese society of at least ¥1.1 trillion ($8 billion) and perhaps as much as ¥2.4 trillion ($17 billion). Even the upper end of this range might understate the impact of trade barriers on the Japanese economy for three reasons. First, and least important, we have only examined a subset of protected products: those which satisfy minimum criteria of a 5 percent unit value differential and imports of at least ¥1 billion. These cutoff criteria inevitably ignore some protected products. Second, the costs to Japan are measured only in terms of static effects and do not reflect the dynamic costs of trade protection; these costs include collusive behavior by firms and slower technical progress. Finally, our estimates ignore the social costs incurred as a consequence of rent-seeking activities that flourish when trade protection is dispensed by public policy or private practice.

Protection is often justified as a means of preserving domestic jobs. Our study finds that this rationale is weak. Japanese restrictions may preserve 0.3 percent of total Japanese jobs, but the jobs saved in protected low-productivity sectors could be replaced by better jobs in high-productivity sectors if Japanese trade barriers were removed. Moreover, jobs preserved by import protection impose an enormous cost on Japanese consumers: over ¥80 million (about $600,000) per job saved and perhaps as much as ¥118 million (about $850,000).

APPENDICES

Estimation of Unit Value Differentials and Sensitivity Analysis of Results

To obtain differentials between domestic producers' unit values and import unit values for each product category in 1989, we first estimated unit value differentials for 1985. We then constructed unit value differentials for 1989 by using product category price deflators that link 1985 and 1989 prices. At three separate stages we applied sensitivity analysis to the results: first, for the calculation of 1985 unit value differentials; second, for the calculation of 1989 deflators; and finally, for the calculation of 1989 unit value differentials.

Unit Value Differentials for 1985

The most recent year for which volume and value data for very disaggregated commodity items are available, for both domestic goods and imports, is 1985. These detailed data were carefully aggregated into similar product categories and unit value differentials were calculated as described below. We interpret the differentials at the product category level as a measure of the tariff equivalent of both tariff and nontariff barriers that restrict foreign access to the Japanese market.

To calculate product category differentials we began with individual domestic items identified at a 10-digit level of input-output classification. If necessary, closely-related items were grouped together into a single commodity and a unit value was calculated by dividing the sum of the item values by the sum of the item quantities. A similar process produced commodity-level unit values for the import items. Each of the domestic commodity unit values was then matched with the unit value for the basket of imported items believed to be close substitutes for it. The difference between these two unit values was then calculated. Any domestic item that could not be matched with at least one similar import was placed in a miscellaneous commodity class; the same was true for imported items that did not match up with any domestic items. For further aggregation purposes, items in the miscellaneous commodity classes were ignored.

Using the unit value differentials for commodity classes, equation (A.1) was used to aggregate unit value differentials (in percentage terms) at the product category level:

$$100 \times [(Pd - Pm)/Pm]_{85} = 100 \times \Sigma W_i[(Pd_i - Pm_i)/Pm_i]_{85}, \quad (A.1)$$

where Pd and Pm stand for, respectively, the unit value of the domestic good and the unit value of the imported good; Pd_i and Pm_i stand for, respectively, the unit value of the domestic good and the unit value of the imported good in the ith commodity class; and W_i is the function used to weight the ith commodity class in calculating the product category unit value level.

The function W_i was defined in two different ways:

$$W_i(1^*) = (Vd_i + Vm_i)/(\Sigma Vd_i + \Sigma Vm_i) \quad (A.2)$$

$$W_i(2^*) = 1/I, \quad (A.3)$$

where:

$W_i(1^*)$ uses the value weight of commodity i in product category j
$[\Sigma W_i(1^*) = 1.00]$
Vd_i and Vm_i are the values, respectively, of domestic and imported commodities in set i in 1985
$W_i(2^*)$ is an alternative weighting system that gives equal weight to each commodity within a product category, where I is equal to the number of commodity classes.

Items placed in the same commodity group had to share a common unit of measurement (e.g., kilograms, number of bottles, meters) and had to be judged similar in nature; for instance, a bottle of cooking oil would not be grouped with a bottle of water. Certain domestic commodity groups were excluded because we could find no imported goods belonging to those groups (and conversely for certain imported commodity groups). In such cases the relevant product categories do not contain all their constituent commodity groups. The last two columns of table A.1 indicate the extent to which commodities are included within each product category. For 30 categories the domestic product coverage ratio is 100 percent; for the remaining 22 categories the domestic product coverage ratio is less than 100 percent. Likewise, for 32 categories the imported product coverage ratio is 100 percent; for the remaining 20 categories the imported product coverage ratio is less than 100 percent.

Table A.1 shows the results of the calculation of unit value differentials for 1985 by product category, following the method indicated by equation (A.1). The results from using value weights, $W_i(1^*)$, are shown in the column labeled "Value weights." These are the preferred results, since a value-weighting scheme accords with the common sense of giving greater weight to items that play a larger economic role within a product category.

To carry out sensitivity analysis we had to devise a weighting scheme that was a plausible variant of the preferred weighting scheme. The point of sensitivity analysis is to see how much the results are affected by a modest change in one of the underlying assumptions—in this case, the scheme for weighting unit value differentials calculated at a commodity level. For this purpose, table A.1 also gives 1985 unit value differentials for each product category based on a second weighting scheme indicated by $W_i(2^*)$, namely, a simple average of unit value differentials for individual commodity groups within each product category.

Our simple sensitivity analysis consists of examining the following ratio:

$$[(Pd/Pm)_{85}, \text{ using } W_i(1^*)]/[(Pd/Pm)_{85}, \text{ using } W_i(2^*)]. \qquad (A.4)$$

If the ratio described by equation (A.4) is less than 0.75 or greater than 1.33, we characterize the 1985 unit value differential as highly unstable. We characterize ratio values between 0.75 and 0.85, or between 1.18 and 1.33, as moderately unstable. Next, we characterize ratio values between 0.85 and 0.95, or between 1.05 and 1.18, as moderately stable. Finally, we characterize ratio values between 0.95 and 1.05 as highly stable.

On the basis of this characterization schedule, our sensitivity analysis yields the following results for product categories containing more than one commodity group (see table A.1):[1]

- highly unstable 1985 unit value differentials: 1 product category, accounting for 0.1 percent of 1989 imports listed in table 1.1

- moderately unstable 1985 unit value differentials: 5 product categories, accounting for 16.9 percent of 1989 imports listed in table 1.1

---

1. This discussion excludes five product categories that did not qualify as protected sectors in 1989, but nevertheless are included in the appendix A tables for the sake of information, because they have been the subject of trade controversy: other sugar and by-products, paperboard, crude petroleum, heavy oil A, and agricultural machinery.

Table A.1 Unit value differentials, 1985

Sector and product category	Unit value differentials based on:[a]		Pd/Pm based on:[b]		Sensitivity analysis[c]		Domestic coverage (percentages)[d]	Import coverage (percentages)[e]
	Value weights	Simple average	Value weights	Simple average	Ratio	Characterization		
Food and beverages								
Wheat	355.1	355.1	4.551	4.551	1.000	Not applicable	100.0	100.0
Soybeans	338.3	338.3	4.383	4.383	1.000	Not applicable	100.0	100.0
Citrus fruits[f]	85.3	85.3	1.853	1.853	1.000	Not applicable	100.0	100.0
Oilseeds other than soybeans	214.0	252.5	3.140	3.525	0.891	Moderately stable	98.3	80.0
Leaf tobacco	123.0	123.0	2.230	2.230	1.000	Not applicable	100.0	100.0
Dressed carcasses (beef, pork, etc.) and poultry	8.9	7.6	1.089	1.076	1.012	Highly stable	100.0	97.8
Processed meat products	64.5	64.5	1.645	1.645	1.000	Not applicable	100.0	100.0
Dairy products	267.5	225.6	3.675	3.256	1.129	Moderately stable	44.4	86.3
Milled rice	587.5	587.5	6.875	6.875	1.000	Not applicable	100.0	100.0
Bread	318.9	318.9	4.189	4.189	1.000	Not applicable	100.0	100.0
Confectionery goods	88.8	95.3	1.888	1.953	0.967	Highly stable	54.0	85.2
Canned or bottled vegetables and fruits	56.6	51.5	1.566	1.515	1.034	Highly stable	100.0	99.6
Beer	92.6	92.6	1.926	1.926	1.000	Not applicable	99.9	100.0
Whiskey and brandy	208.4	174.7	3.084	2.747	1.123	Moderately stable	100.0	100.0
Tea and roasted coffee	355.1	387.7	4.551	4.877	0.933	Moderately stable	73.5	59.9
Sparkling and still beverages	82.7	82.7	1.827	1.827	1.000	Not applicable	100.0	100.0
Tobacco products	164.4	164.4	2.644	2.644	1.000	Not applicable	100.0	22.7
Other sugar and by-products[g]	16.4	71.3	1.164	1.713	0.680	Highly unstable	100.0	70.7
Textiles and light industries								
Cotton yarn	26.3	26.3	1.263	1.263	1.000	Not applicable	100.0	98.6
Knit fabrics	2.5	-2.1	1.025	0.979	1.047	Highly stable	84.6	82.8

Clothing	307.3	208.1	4.073	3.081	1.322	Moderately unstable	26.9	97.5
Plywood	20.6	20.6	1.206	1.206	1.000	Not applicable	100.0	91.0
Paper	14.7	-8.9	1.147	0.911	1.259	Moderately unstable	32.4	17.2
Leather footwear[h]	-24.4	-13.8	0.756	0.862	0.877	Moderately stable	87.7	85.3
Paperboard[g,h]	-8.8	-22.0	0.912	0.780	1.169	Moderately stable	94.0	100.0
Metal products								
Copper ore	181.5	181.5	2.815	2.815	1.000	Not applicable	100.0	100.0
Sheet glass[h]	-18.5	-23.7	0.815	0.763	1.068	Moderately stable	100.0	100.0
Clay refractories	114.1	18.1	2.141	1.181	1.813	Highly unstable	68.2	74.5
Ferroalloys	27.4	27.4	1.274	1.274	1.000	Not applicable	99.8	100.0
Lead (incl. regenerated)[i]	87.9	87.9	1.879	1.879	1.000	Not applicable	100.4	100.0
Regenerated aluminum	27.1	27.1	1.271	1.271	1.000	Not applicable	100.0	100.0
Other nonferrous metals	3.4	26.9	1.034	1.269	0.815	Moderately unstable	48.0	71.0
Chemical products								
Natural gas	5.5	5.5	1.055	1.055	1.000	Not applicable	99.9	100.0
Nitric fertilizers	62.0	92.3	1.620	1.923	0.842	Moderately unstable	80.4	86.5
Soda ash	77.3	77.3	1.773	1.773	1.000	Not applicable	100.0	100.0
Caustic soda	203.9	203.9	3.039	3.039	1.000	Not applicable	100.0	100.0
Titanium oxide	34.2	34.2	1.342	1.342	1.000	Not applicable	99.1	100.0
Methane derivatives	104.7	104.7	2.047	2.047	1.000	Not applicable	95.5	100.0
Industrial oil and fat	12.5	12.5	1.125	1.125	1.000	Not applicable	85.9	100.0
Polyethylene	32.5	31.6	1.325	1.316	1.007	Highly stable	100.0	100.0
Pharmaceuticals[i]	0.0	0.0	1.000	1.000	1.000	Not applicable	100.0	100.0
Cosmetics, toilet preparations	646.6	641.3	7.466	7.413	1.007	Highly stable	61.5	69.8
Gasoline[i]	51.0	51.0	1.510	1.510	1.000	Not applicable	100.3	100.0
Crude petroleum[g]	9.4	9.4	1.094	1.094	1.000	Not applicable	100.0	100.0
Heavy oil A[g]	14.8	14.8	1.148	1.148	1.000	Not applicable	100.0	74.1
Machinery								
Chemical machinery[i]	0.0	0.0	1.000	1.000	1.000	Not applicable	100.0	100.0
Radio and television sets[i]	247.5	191.0	3.475	2.910	1.194	Moderately unstable	100.3	100.0
Electric computing equipment	32.9	28.8	1.329	1.288	1.032	Highly stable	82.2	100.0
Communication equipment	312.5	318.1	4.125	4.181	0.987	Highly stable	31.2	38.2
Semiconductor devices	88.5	94.2	1.885	1.942	0.971	Highly stable	94.7	100.0

continued next page

Table A.1 Unit value differentials, 1985 (continued)

Sector and product category	Unit value differentials based on:[a]		Pd/Pm based on:[b]		Sensitivity analysis[c]		Domestic coverage (percentages)[d]	Import coverage (percentages)[e]
	Value weights	Simple average	Value weights	Simple average	Ratio	Characterization		
Machinery (continued)								
Medical instruments[j]	0.0	0.0	1.000	1.000	1.000	Not applicable	100.0	100.0
Agricultural machinery[f,g,h]	−30.2	−30.2	0.698	0.698	1.000	Not applicable	100.0	100.0

a. Unit value differentials are symbolically defined as $100 \times [(Pd - Pm)/Pm]$. They are calculated in accordance with equation (A.1) in the text using, respectively, value weights according to equation (A.2) and simple averages according to equation (A.3). The differentials are interpreted as the tariff equivalent of tariffs plus nontariff barriers.

b. The value of Pd/Pm is found by adding 100.0 to the respective unit value differential, and then dividing by 100.0.

c. The sensitivity ratio is the ratio between two different calculations of Pd/Pm. The first is calculated using value weights for individual items; the second is calculated using simple averages. See equation (A.4). The characterization of the sensitivity ratio follows the grading system in appendix A: a "highly stable" value lies between 0.95 and 1.05; a "moderately stable" value lies between 0.85 and 0.95 or between 1.05 and 1.18; a "moderately unstable" value lies between 0.75 and 0.85 or between 1.18 and 1.33; a "highly unstable" value lies below 0.75 or above 1.33. A ratio characterized as "not applicable" indicates that the product category is made up of only one commodity group, so that aggregation is indifferent to the choice of weighting scheme.

d. Proportion of domestic production in the product category represented by domestic commodity items that could be matched to highly similar imported commodity items.

e. Proportion of imports in the product category represented by imported commodity items that could be matched to highly similar domestic commodity items.

f. Since information on unit values is not available from the input-output table, the differentials for these product categories are taken from OECD (1985).

g. One of five product categories that did not pass the screens for inclusion in the evaluation of trade barriers, because the calculated unit value differentials were negative in 1989 (see table A.3). These five categories are shown in the table because they have been the subject of trade controversy in the past.

h. Selected product categories with a value-weighted unit value differential of less than zero have been included in the study, because they have been the subject of trade controversy in the past.

i. As a result of slight disparities in data sources, these categories had calculated domestic coverage percentages of greater than 100.0. In the interest of clarity, these percentages have been forced to 100.0.

j. Since information on unit values is not available either from the input-output table or from OECD (1985), the unit value differentials are assumed to be zero.

Sources: Authors' estimates based on Japanese input-output tables (Management and Coordination Agency 1989 and MITI, various years).

■ moderately stable 1985 unit value differentials: 6 product categories, accounting for 7.6 percent of 1989 imports listed in table 1.1

■ highly stable 1985 unit value differentials: 9 product categories, accounting for 32.3 percent of 1989 imports listed in table 1.1.

It should first be noted that no conclusions about sensitivity can be drawn for the 26 product categories that each consist of only a single commodity group; for these single-commodity categories, the weighting of unit value differentials at a commodity level cannot affect the measurement for the product category.[2] These 26 indeterminate categories, which are *not* included in the summary above, account for 43 percent of 1989 imports in the product categories listed in table 1.1. The food and beverage sector contains 10 of the excluded product categories, where they comprise 10.5 percent of 1989 imports listed in table 1.1. The chemical products sector contains another 8 of the excluded product categories, where they account for 17.6 percent of 1985 imports listed in table 1.1. For product categories in these two sectors, the use of unit values may not lead to an exaggerated evaluation of trade barriers, since it seems unlikely that imports are systematically of lower quality per unit of measurement than domestic goods.

From the first sensitivity exercise, summarized above, we conclude that the estimates of unit value differentials are robust: 71 percent of the product categories susceptible to evaluation can be characterized as either highly or moderately stable. These categories account for 40 percent of Japan's 1989 imports listed in table 1.1. In general, we find that weighting by values does not yield a significantly different evaluation of the 1985 unit value differentials than simple-average weighting for most categories. Some instability does, however, characterize the clothing, paper, clay refractories, other nonferrous metals, nitric fertilizer, and radio and television set product categories.

Price Deflators for 1989

The next step was to extend the calculated 1985 unit value differentials for each product category to the year 1989. This required the development of product category price deflators for both domestic goods and imports. The price deflators for 1989 (with 1985 deflators = 1.000) are shown in table A.2.

---

2. A single-commodity product category may in fact contain more than one commodity group. The designation only refers to the number of commodities covered in this study. The absence of similar domestic and imported items may cause a product category with several commodity groups to be represented by only one in this study.

Table A.2 Price deflators, 1989 (1985 = 1.000)

Sector and product category	MITI estimates		Our estimates		Sensitivity analysis	
	Pd (M*89)	Pm (M*89)	Pm (1*89)	Pm (2*89)	Ratio	Characterization
Food and beverages						
Wheat	0.873	0.688	0.689	0.689	1.000	Not applicable
Soybeans[d]	0.860	0.720	0.720	0.720	1.000	Not applicable
Citrus fruits[e]	0.926	0.751	0.751	0.751	1.000	Not applicable
Oilseeds other than soybeans	1.323	0.583	0.570	0.572	0.997	Highly stable
Leaf tobacco[d]	1.050	1.066	1.066	1.066	1.000	Not applicable
Dressed carcasses (beef, pork, etc.) and poultry	0.947	0.750	0.744	0.759	0.980	Highly stable
Processed meat products	0.971	0.727	0.734	0.734	1.000	Not applicable
Dairy products	0.989	1.036	1.106	1.100	1.006	Highly stable
Milled rice[d]	0.960	0.789	0.789	0.789	1.000	Not applicable
Bread[d]	1.039	0.975	0.975	0.975	1.000	Not applicable
Confectionery goods	1.016	0.669	0.617	0.726	0.850	Moderately stable
Canned or bottled vegetables and fruits	1.113	0.740	0.729	0.734	0.993	Highly stable
Beer[d]	0.933	0.740	0.740	0.740	1.000	Not applicable
Whiskey and brandy	0.803	1.277	1.352	1.352	1.000	Highly stable
Tea and roasted coffee	0.972	0.564	0.541	0.548	0.987	Highly stable
Sparkling and still beverages	1.026	0.631	0.625	0.625	1.000	Not applicable
Tobacco products	1.105	0.702	0.857	0.857	1.000	Not applicable
Other sugar and by-products	0.918	1.164	1.458	1.464	0.996	Highly stable
Textiles and light industries						
Cotton yarn	0.752	0.678	0.680	0.680	1.000	Not applicable
Knit fabrics	0.943	0.544	0.895	0.886	1.010	Highly stable
Clothing	1.083	0.868	1.124	1.137	0.989	Highly stable
Plywood	1.065	0.947	0.983	0.983	1.000	Not applicable
Paper	0.931	0.643	0.874	0.877	0.997	Highly stable
Leather footwear	1.083	0.513	0.720	0.641	1.123	Moderately stable
Paperboard	0.836	0.854	0.844	0.885	0.954	Highly stable
Metal products						
Copper ore	0.994	1.080	1.080	1.080	1.000	Not applicable
Sheet glass	1.051	0.525	1.066	0.863	1.235	Moderately unstable
Clay refractories	0.987	0.590	0.754	0.693	1.088	Moderately stable
Ferroalloys	0.891	0.933	0.779	0.779	1.000	Not applicable

	Pd (M*89)	Pm (M*89)	Pm (1*89)	Pm (2*89)	Sensitivity ratio	Characterization
Lead (incl. regenerated)	0.584	0.889	0.707	0.707	1.000	Not applicable
Regenerated aluminum	0.896	0.905	1.046	1.046	1.000	Not applicable
Other nonferrous metals	0.696	0.742	0.635	0.652	0.974	Highly stable
Chemical products						
Natural gas	0.752	0.372	0.372	0.372	1.000	Not applicable
Nitric fertilizers	0.703	0.631	0.616	0.624	0.987	Highly stable
Soda ash	0.820	0.585	1.089	1.089	1.000	Not applicable
Caustic soda	0.876	0.823	0.868	0.868	1.000	Not applicable
Titanium oxide	0.992	0.952	0.959	0.959	1.000	Not applicable
Methane derivatives	0.874	0.611	0.581	0.581	1.000	Not applicable
Industrial oil and fat	0.655	0.510	0.563	0.563	1.000	Not applicable
Polyethylene	0.829	0.825	0.866	0.866	1.000	Highly stable
Pharmaceuticals[e]	0.919	0.847	0.847	0.847	1.000	Not applicable
Cosmetics, toilet preparations	1.003	0.759	0.983	1.017	0.967	Highly stable
Gasoline	0.739	0.339	0.286	0.286	1.000	Not applicable
Crude petroleum	0.294	0.341	0.341	0.341	1.000	Not applicable
Heavy oil A	0.358	0.440	0.428	0.428	1.000	Not applicable
Machinery						
Chemical machinery[e]	1.042	0.647	0.647	0.647	1.000	Not applicable
Radio and television sets	1.236	0.608	0.860	0.640	1.344	Highly unstable
Electric computing equipment	0.876	0.662	0.411	0.415	0.990	Highly stable
Communication equipment	0.709	0.417	0.869	0.757	1.148	Moderately stable
Semiconductor devices	0.909	0.829	1.620	1.652	0.981	Highly stable
Medical instruments[e]	0.958	0.722	0.722	0.722	1.000	Not applicable
Agricultural machinery[e]	1.078	0.743	0.743	0.743	1.000	Not applicable

a. In the MITI estimates Pd (M*89) indicates the domestic price deflator, while Pm (M*89) indicates the import price deflator.

b. In our estimates Pm (1*89) is the import price deflator calculated giving equal weight to each matched commodity set within a product category, while Pm (2*89) is the import price deflator calculated using value weights for matched commodity sets, while Pm (2*89) is the import price deflator calculated giving equal weight to each matched commodity set within a product category.

c. The sensitivity ratio is the ratio between Pm (1*89) and Pm (2*89). See equation (A.5) in the text. The characterization of the ratio follows the grading system in appendix A: a "highly stable" value lies between 0.95 and 1.05; a "moderately stable" value lies between 0.85 and 0.95 or between 1.05 and 1.18; a "moderately unstable" value lies between 0.75 and 0.85 or between 1.18 and 1.33; a "highly unstable" value lies below 0.75 or above 1.33. A ratio characterized as "not applicable" indicates that the product category is made up of only one commodity group, so that aggregation is indifferent to the choice of weighting scheme.

d. The MITI import price deflator was used for Pm (1*89).

e. Information to calculate import price deflators was not available, and the deflators are instead taken from OECD (1985).

Sources: Pd (M*89) and Pm (M*89) from MITI (1992). All other data are estimated by the authors, based on disaggregated import data (Japan Tariff Association 1990).

The first two columns of table A.2 show the 1989 MITI price deflators for each domestic product category and for each import product category. For domestic products only the price deflators reported by MITI were available, and accordingly these were used.

However, we did not generally use the MITI import price deflators, because we wanted the weighting of our import price deflators to correspond closely with the weighting of items that were included within each product category. For these purposes it was usually possible to improve on the MITI import price deflators. We did, however, use the MITI deflators (and sometimes OECD deflators) when the alternative calculation was not possible.

Our "improved" deflators were calculated to reflect the price experience of the included items within each product category, using the same weights that were used to calculate unit value differentials. This was done as follows. Information on imports at a disaggregated level for 1989 are available from the Japan Tariff Association (1990). Using these data we computed 1989 unit import values for all commodities; these values were compared with 1985 values to obtain price deflators for each commodity. We then aggregated the commodity deflators in the usual way by value weights to construct deflators at the product category level.

To be consistent both with the 1985 unit value differentials reported in table A.1, and with MITI price deflators for domestic products reported in table A.2, our import price deflators were also calculated using 1985 value weights. These are indicated by $Pm(1^*89)$ in table A.2.

It will be observed that the MITI import price deflators shown in table A.2 are very similar to the $Pm(1^*89)$ price deflators. This is not surprising, given that the coverage ratio normally exceeds 50 percent, and given the similar weighting scheme used to calculate both sets of deflators.

For purposes of sensitivity analysis, a plausible alternative weighting scheme was devised to calculate price deflators: in the alternative scheme we used 1989 value weights rather than 1985 value weights. These alternative price deflators are indicated by $Pm(2^*89)$ in table A.2. Our sensitivity analysis consists of examining the ratio between the two price deflators:

$$Pm(1^*89)/Pm(2^*89). \qquad (A.5)$$

For the 26 indeterminate product categories mentioned in the previous section, the two price deflators $Pm(1^*89)$ and $Pm(2^*89)$ are the same, because there was only one commodity group included in each category. As a result, the weighting scheme does not affect the calculated deflator, since both schemes will accord the single commodity group a weight of 100 percent. Ignoring these 26 product categories, we can sort the remaining categories into grades according to the ratio values. We characterize the ratios in four grades, ranging from highly unstable to highly stable, based on the same tests used earlier. The results are as follows:

■ highly unstable price deflators: 1 product category, accounting for just 0.6 percent of 1989 imports listed in table 1.1

■ moderately unstable price deflators: 1 product category, accounting for just 0.5 percent of 1989 imports listed in table 1.1

■ moderately stable price deflators: 4 product categories, accounting for 2.5 percent of 1989 imports listed in table 1.1

■ highly stable price deflators: 15 product categories, accounting for 53.4 percent of 1989 imports listed in table 1.1.

This second sensitivity exercise suggests that the price deflator estimates are robust, since only one product category, radio and television sets, can be characterized as highly unstable, and one category, sheet glass, can be characterized as moderately unstable. It appears that, in computing the import price deflator, a change from 1985 value weights to 1989 value weights makes no discernible difference in the results.

Unit Value Differentials for 1989

For each product category we calculated unit value differentials for 1989 by adjusting the 1985 differentials using the calculated import price deflator and the MITI domestic price deflator for that category. The formula for deriving the preferred 1989 differentials, which appear both in table 1.1 and in the first column of table A.3, is:

Alternative one:

$$100 \times [(Pd - Pm)/Pm]_{89 \cdot 1} =$$

$$\{100 \times [Pd/Pm]_{85} Wi(1^*) \times [Pd(M^*89)/Pm(1^*89)]\} - 100, \qquad (A.6)$$

where:

$100 \times [(Pd/Pm)]_{85} Wi(1^*)$ represents the value-weighted ratio of domestic and import unit values in 1985, expressed as a percentage (this magnitude may be found by adding 100.0 to the differentials reported in the first column of table A.1)

Pd and Pm are, respectively, the domestic and imported unit values, and $W_i(1^*)$ is a value-weighting function

Table A.3 Unit value differentials, 1989

Sector and product category	Unit value differentials based on:[a]				Sensitivity analysis[b]	
	Value weights and Pm (1*89)	Simple average and Pm (1*89)	Value weights and Pm (2*89)	Simple average and Pm (2*89)	Ratio	Characterization
Food and beverages						
Wheat	477.8	477.8	477.8	477.8	1.000	Not applicable
Soybeans	423.6	423.6	423.6	423.6	1.000	Not applicable
Citrus fruits	128.5	128.5	128.5	128.5	1.000	Not applicable
Oilseeds other than soybeans	628.6	717.9	626.5	715.6	0.891	Moderately stable
Leaf tobacco	119.6	119.6	119.6	119.6	1.000	Not applicable
Dressed carcasses (beef, pork, etc.) and poultry	38.6	36.9	35.7	34.1	1.034	Highly stable
Processed meat products	119.8	119.8	119.8	119.8	1.000	Not applicable
Dairy products	228.6	191.1	230.3	192.6	1.129	Moderately stable
Milled rice	737.1	737.1	737.1	737.1	1.000	Not applicable
Bread	346.5	346.5	346.5	346.5	1.000	Not applicable
Confectionery goods	210.8	221.5	164.4	173.5	1.175	Moderately stable
Canned or bottled vegetables and fruits	139.2	131.4	137.6	129.9	1.040	Highly stable
Beer	143.0	143.0	143.0	143.0	1.000	Not applicable
Whiskey and brandy	94.1	72.9	94.1	72.9	1.123	Moderately stable
Tea and roasted coffee	718.4	777.0	707.8	765.7	0.933	Moderately stable
Sparkling and still beverages	197.0	197.0	197.0	197.0	1.000	Not applicable
Tobacco products	241.2	241.2	241.2	241.2	1.000	Not applicable
Other sugar and by-products[c]	−26.7	7.8	−27.0	7.4	0.680	Highly unstable
Textiles and light industries						
Cotton yarn	39.6	39.6	39.6	39.6	1.000	Not applicable
Knit fabrics	8.1	3.2	9.1	4.2	1.047	Highly stable
Clothing	292.6	197.0	288.0	193.5	1.338	Highly unstable
Plywood	30.7	30.7	30.7	30.7	1.000	Not applicable
Paper	22.1	−2.9	21.8	−3.2	1.261	Moderately unstable
Leather footwear	13.8	29.8	27.7	45.6	0.782	Moderately unstable
Paperboard[c]	−10.7	−23.6	−10.7	−23.6	1.169	Moderately stable
Metal products						
Copper ore	159.2	159.2	159.2	159.2	1.000	Not applicable
Sheet glass	63.1	52.7	63.1	52.7	1.068	Moderately stable

Clay refractories	180.3	54.7	205.1	68.3	1.812	Highly unstable
Ferroalloys	21.6	21.6	21.6	21.6	1.000	Not applicable
Lead (incl. regenerated)	23.4	23.4	23.4	23.4	1.000	Not applicable
Regenerated aluminum	25.9	25.9	25.9	25.9	1.000	Not applicable
Other nonferrous metals	13.5	39.2	10.5	35.5	0.815	Moderately unstable
Chemical products						
Natural gas	113.4	113.4	113.4	113.4	1.000	Not applicable
Nitric fertilizers	84.8	119.4	82.5	116.6	0.842	Moderately unstable
Soda ash	148.5	148.5	148.5	148.5	1.000	Not applicable
Caustic soda	223.7	223.7	223.7	223.7	1.000	Not applicable
Titanium oxide	39.8	39.8	39.8	39.8	1.000	Not applicable
Methane derivatives	193.0	193.0	193.0	193.0	1.000	Not applicable
Industrial oil and fat	44.7	44.7	44.7	44.7	1.000	Not applicable
Polyethylene	33.2	32.2	33.2	32.2	1.008	Highly stable
Pharmaceuticals	8.5	8.5	8.5	8.5	1.000	Not applicable
Cosmetics, toilet preparations	661.6	656.3	635.8	630.7	1.042	Highly stable
Gasoline	229.0	229.0	229.0	229.0	1.000	Not applicable
Crude petroleum[c]	−5.8	−5.8	−5.8	−5.8	1.000	Not applicable
Heavy oil A[c]	−3.9	−3.9	−3.9	−3.9	1.000	Not applicable
Machinery						
Chemical machinery	61.1	61.1	61.1	61.1	1.000	Not applicable
Radio and television sets	607.0	492.0	607.0	492.0	1.190	Moderately unstable
Electric computing equipment	75.8	70.4	75.8	70.4	1.032	Highly stable
Communication equipment	236.6	241.2	286.3	291.5	0.860	Moderately stable
Semiconductor devices	106.6	112.8	106.6	112.8	0.971	Highly stable
Medical instruments	32.7	32.7	32.7	32.7	1.000	Not applicable
Agricultural machinery[c]	1.3	1.3	1.3	1.3	1.000	Not applicable

a. The alternative unit value differentials are calculated in accordance with equations (A.6), (A.7), (A.8), and (A.9) in the text. The preferred differentials are in the first column, based on equation (A.6).

b. The sensitivity ratio is the minimum or maximum ratio between the value of Pd/Pm embedded in the preferred differential reported in the first column and the most disparate value of Pd/Pm embedded in one of the next three columns. The characterization of the sensitivity ratio follows the grading system in appendix A: a "highly stable" value lies between 0.95 and 1.05; a "moderately stable" value lies between 0.85 and 0.95 or between 1.05 and 1.18; a "moderately unstable" value lies between 0.75 and 0.85 or between 1.18 and 1.33; a "highly unstable" value lies below 0.75 or above 1.33. A ratio characterized as not applicable indicates that the product category is made up of only one commodity group, so that aggregation is indifferent to the choice of weighting scheme.

c. One of five product categories that did not pass the screens for inclusion in the evaluation of trade barriers, because the calculated unit value differentials were negative or less than 5 percent in 1989 (see the first column in the table). These five categories are shown in the table because they have been the subject of trade controversy in the past.

Sources: Based on data reported in tables A.1 and A.2.

Pd(M*89) is the 1989 MITI domestic price deflator for the given product
category

Pm(1*89) is the preferred import price deflator, using 1985 value weights,
whose calculation is explained in the previous section.

In addition to the preferred formula (A.6), three variations were calculated for the purposes of sensitivity analysis:

Alternative two:

$$100 \times [(Pd-Pm)/Pm]_{89 \cdot 2} =$$

$$\{100 \times [Pd/Pm]_{85} W_i(2^*) \times [Pd(\text{M}^*89)/Pm(1^*89)]\} - 100 \qquad \text{(A.7)}$$

Alternative three:

$$100 \times [(Pd-Pm)/Pm]_{89 \cdot 3} =$$

$$\{100 \times [Pd/Pm]_{85} W_i(1^*) \times [Pd(\text{M}^*89)/Pm(2^*89)]\} - 100 \qquad \text{(A.8)}$$

Alternative four:

$$100 \times [(Pd-Pm)/Pm]_{89 \cdot 4} =$$

$$\{100 \times [Pd/Pm]_{85} W_i(2^*) \times [Pd(\text{M}^*89)/Pm(2^*89)]\} - 100, \qquad \text{(A.9)}$$

where:

$W_i(2^*)$ is a simple average weighting function

Pm(2*89) is the alternative import price deflator, using 1989 value weights.

Our sensitivity analysis consists of finding the minimum or maximum
ratio between our preferred calculation of the 1989 unit value differential for each product category, formula (A.6), plus 100, and the most
disparate alternative, formula (A.7) or (A.8) or (A.9), plus 100, as the case
may be.[3] Once again it should be noted that 26 categories were not
covered by this sensitivity analysis, because they are each made up of a
single commodity group. We characterize the minimum or maximum
ratio in the remaining categories as belonging to one of four grades,
based on the same tests used earlier. The results of this sensitivity analysis, reported in table A.3, are as follows:

---

3. The ratio between the domestic price and the import price, $100 \times Pd/Pm$, is used for
the sensitivity analysis because using the unit value differentials tends to overstate the
sensitivity of estimates that are close to zero. This requires adding 100 to the unit value
differential estimates in table A.3.

- Highly unstable 1989 unit value differentials: 2 product categories, accounting for 8.0 percent of 1989 imports listed in table 1.1

- Moderately unstable 1989 unit value differentials: 5 product categories, accounting for 9.5 percent of 1989 imports listed in table 1.1

- Moderately stable 1989 unit value differentials: 7 product categories, accounting for 9.1 percent of 1989 imports listed in table 1.1

- Highly stable 1989 unit value differentials: 7 product categories, accounting for 30.4 percent of 1989 imports listed in table 1.1.

From this third and most important sensitivity analysis we may conclude that our estimates are relatively robust, since we can characterize 14 of the 21 relevant product categories as stable, and these make up almost 40 percent of 1989 imports listed in table 1.1. As before, it seems that the choice of weighting scheme does not affect the calculated 1989 unit value differentials in most cases. However, the calculations for clothing, paper, leather footwear, clay refractories, other nonferrous metals, nitric fertilizers, and radio and television sets must be treated with caution, since they do exhibit some instability.

Derivation of Supply Elasticities

In this study, Japanese domestic supply elasticities (E_s) were estimated according to the following reduced-form equation:

$$E_s = E_{dd} + (E_{dm}/\Gamma), \text{ where } \Gamma = \partial(\ln Pd)/\partial(\ln Pm), \qquad \text{(B.1)}$$

where:

E_{dd} = own-price elasticity of domestic demand
E_{dm} = cross-price elasticity of domestic demand with respect to the price of imports
Pd = domestic product price
Pm = imported product price, c.i.f.
$\partial(\ln Pd)/\partial(\ln Pm)$ represents the partial derivative of $\ln Pd$ with respect to $\ln Pm$.

Equation (B.1) was derived from a structural model of a partial equilibrium system defined by two equations, one a multiplicative demand function with constant term a, and the other a multiplicative supply function with constant term b. These are the same as the demand and supply functions specified in appendix C:

$$Qd = aPd^{Edd}Pm^{Edm} \qquad \text{(B.2)}$$

$$Qs = bPd^{Es}. \qquad \text{(B.3)}$$

Taking the natural logarithms of equations (B.2) and (B.3), we obtained:

$$\ln Qd = \ln a + E_{dd}\ln Pd + E_{dm}\ln Pm \tag{B.4}$$

$$\ln Qs = \ln b + E_s\ln Pd. \tag{B.5}$$

We assume that commodity markets are in equilibrium, and thus the quantity supplied equals the quantity demanded. This condition in turn implies that the natural logarithm of quantity supplied equals the natural logarithm of quantity demanded. Hence, equation (B.4) may be set equal to equation (B.5), resulting in:

$$0 = \ln(a/b) + (E_{dd} - E_s)\ln Pd + E_{dm}\ln Pm. \tag{B.6}$$

Finally, taking the partial derivative of equation (B.6) with respect to $\ln Pm$ gives us the following expression:

$$0 = (E_{dd} - E_s)[(\partial(\ln Pd)/\partial(\ln Pm)] + E_{dm}. \tag{B.7}$$

Equation (B.7) may be transformed with basic arithmetic manipulation into equation (B.1) by isolating E_s on the lefthand side of the equation. The estimates of E_s using equation (B.1) required information on demand elasticities (E_{dd} and E_{dm}) and ($\partial(\ln Pd)/\partial(\ln Pm)$). The demand elasticities are taken from table 3.1; values for $\partial(\ln Pd)/\partial(\ln Pm)$ were separately calculated by the authors (for further information contact Hiroki Kawai; see p. iv).

To estimate the partial equilibrium models in appendix C we also required values for $\ln a$ and $\ln b$. We solved equation (B.5) for $\ln b$ using the estimated supply elasticities and input-output data on price and quantity. Because of the conventions we used in defining prices at the equilibrium point, it turns out that $\ln a$ equals $\ln b$ for the following two reasons. First, quantity units are defined so that all prices in equilibrium equal one. Second, in equilibrium Qd equals Qs; hence, from equations (B.2) and (B.3), a must equal b. In turn, this means that $\ln a$ equals $\ln b$.

A Computable Partial Equilibrium Model

This appendix outlines the simple comparative static framework used in this study for calculating the welfare effects of trade barriers.[1] The framework is similar to that found in Morkre and Tarr (1980) and Tarr and Morkre (1984); it is founded on a partial equilibrium analysis with four key assumptions:

- the domestic good and the imported good are imperfect substitutes;

- the supply schedule for the imported good is flat (perfectly elastic);

- the supply schedule for the domestic good is upwardly sloped (less than perfectly elastic);

- all markets are perfectly competitive.

The effects of removing a trade barrier (either a tariff or a quota) under these assumptions are illustrated in figures C.1 and C.2. For example, elimination of a tariff lowers the barrier-inclusive price of the import in the domestic market from Pm to Pm' in figure C.1.[2] In figure

---

1. This appendix is taken from Hufbauer and Elliott, (1994, 31–37). It is based on a computable partial equilibrium model designed by Peter Uimonen when he was a research assistant at the Institute for International Economics. Mr. Uimonen is currently an economist at the International Monetary Fund.

2. The notation in this appendix and in figures C.1 and C.2 is different from that in the rest of the book, where Pm represents the c.i.f. import price or unit value. Here, Pm refers to the c.i.f. import price plus the tariff and tariff equivalent of nontariff barriers.

Figure C.1 Effects in the import market of removing a trade barrier

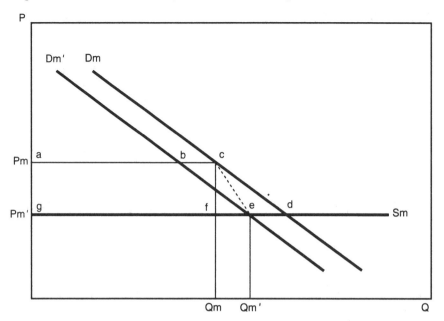

With the trade barrier in place, the price of the import in the protected market is *Pm*, and the quantity imported is *Qm*. Following liberalization, the price falls to *Pm'*, the world price. Then, responding to a lower price in the domestic market (see figure C.2), the demand schedule for the import shifts from *Dm* to *Dm'*, and the quantity imported settles at *Qm'*.

C.2 the decrease in the price of the imported good causes an inward shift in the demand curve for the domestic commodity from *Dd* to *Dd'*. This in turn leads to a decrease in the price of the domestic product from *Pd* to *Pd'*.

Returning to figure C.1, the decrease in the domestic price causes the demand schedule for the imported good to shift from *Dm* to *Dm'*. When equilibrium is restored, prices of both the imported good and the domestic good are lower, output of the domestically produced good is also lower (by the difference between *Qd* and *Qd'*), and the quantity of imports is higher (by the difference between *Qm* and *Qm'*).[3]

Calculating the Welfare Effects of Trade Barriers

The changes in prices and quantities due to trade liberalization result in a gain in consumer surplus, both in the import market and in the do-

---

3. The same story could be told if the initial liberalization was to increase an import quota from *Qm* to *Qm'*. Then the system would work back to lower import prices.

Figure C.2 Effects in the domestic market of removing a trade barrier

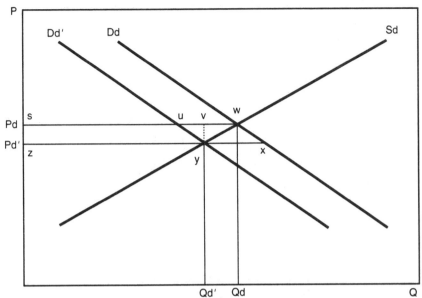

With the trade barrier in place, the price of the import-competing domestic product is *Pd*, and the quantity demanded is *Qd*. Following liberalization and the decline in the import price (see figure C.1), demand for the domestic substitute falls, shifting the demand curve from *Dd* to *Dd'*, the quantity consumed falls to *Qd'*, and the price drops to *Pd'*.

mestic market. Part of the gain arises because consumers now pay less for a good than they paid when supply was restricted. In addition, some consumers who previously were priced out of the market entirely will now enter the market. The consumer surplus gain due to liberalization, however, is partially offset by a loss in producer surplus in the market for the domestic substitute, where prices and output both fall.

If the trade restraint took the form of a tariff, then the revenue lost by the government would also partially offset the consumer gain. If instead a nontariff barrier such as an import quota were used, liberalization would eliminate the rents that previously went to domestic importers.[4] Finally, there would be an efficiency gain because the trade restraint resulted in a misallocation of resources. Before liberalization, the wedge created between the domestic price of the import and the world price caused a transfer of resources toward production of the import substitute and away from other sectors where those resources could have been used more efficiently.

---

4. In Japan, unlike the United States, domestic importers generally capture the quota rents that arise from nontariff barriers.

The methodology used here to quantify these welfare effects is based on Morkre and Tarr (1980). Because the imported and domestic goods are imperfect substitutes, the total gain to consumers must be calculated as the sum of the consumer surplus gain in the two separate markets. Morkre and Tarr estimate that the consumer surplus gain from liberalization in the import market is approximated by the area bounded by points *aceg* (figure C.1). This method of estimating the consumer gain in the import market follows from the analysis of Burns (1973) on the measurement of consumer surplus and gives an average of the consumer gains calculated separately from the two demand curves.[5] Using the old demand schedule (*Dm*) gives the area marked *acdg* as the change in consumer surplus, while the new demand schedule (*Dm'*) gives the area marked *abeg*. The difference between the two areas is shown by the parallelogram marked *bcde*. Line *ce* divides the area in half and gives the compromise consumer surplus change, area *aceg*. Area *aceg* can be estimated by adding rectangle *acfg* to triangle *cef*.

If the form of the protection is a tariff, the rectangular area *acfg* represents a transfer from the government to consumers in the form of lost tariff revenues, and may be estimated as:

$$(Pm - Pm') \times (Qm). \tag{C.1}$$

The area of the triangle marked *cef* represents recovery of the deadweight efficiency loss, which may be estimated as:

$$(1/2) \times [(Pm - Pm') \times (Qm' - Qm)]. \tag{C.2}$$

If nontariff barriers are used, then area *acfg* represents a transfer from importers and distributors (who controlled the domestic market) to consumers. In either case, the consumer gain in the import market equals the sum of rectangle *acfg* and triangle *cef*. If both tariffs and nontariff barriers are imposed, the tariff equivalent of nontariff barriers is assumed to be the difference between the total decline in the import price (*Pm −
Pm'*) and the price effect of the tariff.[6]

We turn next to the effects in the market for the domestically produced good (figure C.2). The consumer welfare gain from lower domestic prices may be approximated by the area marked *swyz*. Area *swyz* can be estimated by adding rectangle *svyz* and triangle *vwy*. This amounts to:

$$(Pd - Pd') \times (Qd') + (1/2) \times [(Pd - Pd') \times (Qd - Qd')]. \tag{C.3}$$

---

5. See Jones (1993) for a mathematical proof of the validity of this method.

6. The price effect of the tariff is normally calculated as *Pm'* times the ad valorem tariff rate.

In the domestic market, the consumer surplus gain is just offset by the producer surplus loss.

Applying the Model

To apply the analysis to particular cases, a simple computable partial equilibrium model was devised corresponding to the graphical analysis above. The form of the model chosen assumes that demand and supply relationships are not linear in absolute terms, but rather are linear in terms of their logarithms (log-linear). This assumption enables the parameters associated with the price terms to be interpreted as elasticities.

To achieve this result, it is necessary to specify the underlying domestic demand and supply functions according to the following forms:

$$Qd = aPd^{Edd}Pm^{Edm} \qquad (C.4)$$

$$Qs = bPd^{Es}. \qquad (C.5)$$

In equation (C.4) E_{dd} is the own-price elasticity of demand for the domestic commodity, while E_{dm} is the cross-price elasticity of demand for the domestic commodity with respect to the price of the imported commodity.[7] In equation (C.5) E_s is the own-price elasticity of supply of the domestic good. Since the domestic commodity and the import are imperfect substitutes in this model, equilibrium in the domestic market requires that domestic demand equals domestic supply—that is, that Qd equals Qs.

Assuming that the supply of the import is perfectly elastic, the supply and demand equations in the import market are:

$$Qm = cPd^{Emd}Pm^{Emm} \qquad (C.6)$$

$$Pm = Pm''(1 + t). \qquad (C.7)$$

In equation (C.6) E_{md} is the cross-price elasticity of demand for the imported commodity with respect to the price of the domestic com-

---

7. The own-price elasticity of demand for the domestic commodity, E_{dd}, is defined as the percentage change in the quantity demanded for each 1 percent change in the price. Other own-price elasticities are defined in an analogous way. Own-price elasticities are normally negative (i.e., an increase in the price of the domestic good causes a decrease in demand for the domestic good). The cross-price elasticity of demand for the domestic commodity, E_{dm}, is defined as the percentage change in the quantity of the domestic good demanded for each 1 percent change in the price of the imported good. Other cross-price elasticities are defined in a similar way. Cross-price elasticities are normally positive (i.e., an increase in the price of the imported good causes an increase in demand for the domestic good).

modity, while E_{mm} is the own-price elasticity of demand for the imported commodity. Equation (C.7) represents the assumption that the supply of the imported commodity is perfectly elastic, and therefore the world price, Pm'', which equals $Pm/(1 + t)$, is the same no matter what the level of imports.

This system of demand and supply functions may be transformed into a system of linear relationships simply by taking the logarithms to the base e (shown by ln) of equations (C.4), (C.5), (C.6), and (C.7):

$$\ln Qd = \ln a + E_{dd}\ln Pd + E_{dm}\ln Pm \qquad (C.8)$$

$$\ln Qs = \ln b + E_s\ln Pd \qquad (C.9)$$

$$\ln Qm = \ln c + E_{md}\ln Pd + E_{mm}\ln Pm \qquad (C.10)$$

$$\ln Pm = \ln[Pm''(1 + t)]. \qquad (C.11)$$

Estimating the effects of a change in trade protection using this system requires two basic steps. First, price and quantity data are used, together with estimates of the elasticity parameters, to solve equations (C.8), (C.9), and (C.10) for the unobservable constant terms: namely, $\ln a$, $\ln b$, and $\ln c$. These terms represent the effects of other (unobserved) nonprice variables on the demand and supply functions. The crucial assumption in this step is that the base period for which the price and quantity data are collected may be considered an equilibrium period (i.e., a period in which it is reasonable to suppose that Qd is equal to Qs).

The second step is to use the estimates of the intercepts and the elasticity parameters, together with a separately estimated change in either the price or the quantity of the import due to a change in protection, to calculate a new equilibrium and, hence, the comparative static welfare effects of the change.

Suppose, for example, that a tariff is eliminated. By invoking the assumption that $\ln Qd$ equals $\ln Qs$, equations (C.8) and (C.9) may be solved together to yield the new price of the domestic commodity as a function of the new import price:

$$\ln Pd' = (\ln a - \ln b)/(E_s - E_{dd}) + [E_{dm}/(E_s - E_{dd})] \times \ln Pm'. \qquad (C.12)$$

In equation (C.12) $\ln Pm'$ is represented by the previous (base-period) import price (corresponding to Pm in figure C.1) minus the change in the price induced by elimination of the tariff (corresponding to the difference between Pm and Pm' in figure C.1). To facilitate computation, base-period prices (inclusive of the tariff) are assumed equal to index values of 1.00; hence tariff changes can be represented in ad valorem terms where the ad valorem rate is applied to the world price without the tariff, Pm'. For example, elimination of a 15 percent tariff would mean that lnPm' is equal to ln(0.87), that is, to ln(1/1.15). The new import and domestic prices can then be substituted into equations (C.8), (C.9), and (C.10) to yield the new equilibrium quantities of imports and domestic output. The welfare effects of the tariff change may then be computed using equations (C.1), (C.2), and (C.3).

References

Bergsten, C. Fred, and Marcus Noland. 1993. *Reconcilable Differences? United States–Japan Economic Conflict.* Washington: Institute for International Economics.

Burns, Michael E. 1973. "A Note on the Concept and Measure of Consumer's Surplus." *American Economic Review* 63, no. 3: 335–44.

Caves, Richard E., and Matthew B. Krepps. 1993. "Fat: The Displacement of Nonproduction Workers from U.S. Manufacturing Industries." *Brookings Papers on Economic Activity: Microeconomics* 2: 227–88.

Deaton, Angus, and John Muellbauer. 1980. "An Almost Ideal Demand System." *American Economic Review* 70 (June): 312–26.

Edwards, Sebastian. 1993. *Trade, Policy, Exchange Rates and Growth.* NBER Working Papers Series no. 4511. Cambridge, MA: National Bureau of Economic Research.

General Agreement on Tariffs and Trade. 1992. *Trade Policy Review Mechanism, Japan.* Geneva.

General Agreement on Tariffs and Trade. 1993. *News of the Uruguay Round* (11 August).

Hufbauer, Gary Clyde, and Kimberly Ann Elliott. 1994. *Measuring the Costs of Protection in the United States.* Washington: Institute for International Economics.

Hufbauer, Gary Clyde, and Jeffrey J. Schott. 1994. *Western Hemisphere Economic Integration.* Washington: Institute for International Economics.

Ide, T. 1990. "Chusho Ryutsugyo no Yunuhin Katsuyo" [Utilizing Imports in Small and Medium Sized Distributors]. *Chusho Kigyo Kinyu Koko Geppo* (October): 14–19.

Japan Tariff Association. 1985. *Japan Exports and Imports, Commodity and Country.* Tokyo (December).

Japan Tariff Association. 1990. *Japan Exports and Imports, Commodity and Country.* Tokyo (December).

Japan External Trade Organization. 1993. *Sekaito Nihon no Boeki* [White Paper on Trade between the World and Japan]. Tokyo.

Jones, Michael. 1993. "The Geometry of Protectionism in the Imperfect Substitutes Model: A Reminder." *Southern Economic Journal* 60 (July): 235–38.

Kawarada, E. 1993. "Kongo no Sen-i Sangyo oyobi Sono Seisaku no Arikata" [Future of Textile Industry and Policy]. *Shoko Kinyu* (September): 18–25.

Keizai Dantai Rengo Kai [Keidanren, Japan Federation of Economic Organizations]. 1993. *Kiseikanwa no Jisshi Jyokyo no Hyoka to Yobo* [Recommendation and Assessment on Deregulation]. Tokyo.

Management and Coordination Agency. 1989. *1985 Input-Output Table*. Tokyo.

Krugman, Paul. 1984. "Import Protection as Export Promotion." In H. Kierzkowski, *Monopolistic Competition in International Trade.* Oxford: Oxford University Press.

Ministry of Agriculture, Fishery, and Forestry. 1992. *Tokyo oyobi Kaigai Shuyo 5 Toshi niokeru Shuyo Shokuryohin no Kourikakaku Chosakekka no Gaiyo* [A Survey of Retail Prices of Major Food Prices in Tokyo and Five Other Major Cities Overseas]. Tokyo.

Ministry of International Trade and Industry. 1992. *Naigai Kakaku Hikaku Chosa Kekka nitsuite* [On the Results of Comparison of Domestic and Foreign Prices]. Tokyo.

Ministry of International Trade and Industry. 1994. *Sen-i Safeguard Sochi no Toriatsukai ni tsuiteno Teigen* [Propositions on the Use of Safeguards on Textiles]. Tokyo (17 May).

Morkre, Morris, and David G. Tarr. 1980. *Effects of Restrictions on United States Imports: Five Case Studies and Theory*. Bureau of Economics Staff Report. Washington: Federal Trade Commission (June).

Organization for Economic Cooperation and Development. 1985. *Purchasing Power Parities and Real Expenditure*. Paris.

Organization for Economic Cooperation and Development. 1987. *National Policies and Agricultural Trade, Japan*. Paris.

Organization for Economic Cooperation and Development. 1989–90. *Energy Business of OECD Countries*. Paris.

Organization for Economic Cooperation and Development. 1992. *Purchasing Power Parities and Real Expenditure, EKS Results,* vol. 1. Paris.

Organization for Economic Cooperation and Development. 1993. *Agriculture Policies, Markets and Trade*. Paris.

Richardson, J. David. 1989. *Trade Liberalisation with Imperfect Competition: A Survey*. OECD Economic Studies no. 12 (Spring): 7–50.

Romer, P. 1994. "New Goods, Old Theory, and the Welfare Costs of Trade Restrictions." *Journal of Development* 43, no. 1: 5–38.

Tarr, David G., and Morris Morkre. 1984. *Aggregate Costs to the United States of Tariffs and Quotas and Imports: General Tariff Cuts and Removal of Quotas on Automobiles, Steel, Sugar, and Textiles*. Bureau of Economics Staff Report. Washington: Federal Trade Commission (December).

Tyson, Laura D'Andrea. 1992. *Who's Bashing Whom? Trade Conflict in High-Technology Industries*. Washington: Institute for International Economics.

US Department of Commerce. 1989. *The Joint DOC/MITI Price Survey: Methodology and Results*. Washington (December).

Urata, Shujiro. 1993. "Japanese Foreign Direct Investment and Its Effect on Foreign Trade in Asia." In T. Ito and A. O. Krueger, eds., *Trade and Protectionism*. Chicago: University of Chicago Press.

Other Publications from the
Institute for International Economics

POLICY ANALYSES IN INTERNATIONAL ECONOMICS Series

BOOKS

Economic Sanctions Reconsidered (in two volumes)
Economic Sanctions Reconsidered: Supplemental Case Histories
Gary Clyde Hufbauer, Jeffrey J. Schott, and Kimberly Ann Elliott/*1985, 2d ed.*
December 1990

ISBN cloth 0-88132-115-X	928 pp.
ISBN paper 0-88132-105-2	928 pp.

Economic Sanctions Reconsidered: History and Current Policy
Gary Clyde Hufbauer, Jeffrey J. Schott, and Kimberly Ann Elliott/*December 1990*

ISBN cloth 0-88132-136-2	288 pp.
ISBN paper 0-88132-140-0	288 pp.

Pacific Basin Developing Countries: Prospects for the Future
Marcus Noland/*January 1991*

ISBN cloth 0-88132-141-9	250 pp.
ISBN paper 0-88132-081-1	250 pp.

Currency Convertibility in Eastern Europe
John Williamson, editor/*October 1991*

ISBN cloth 0-88132-144-3	396 pp.
ISBN paper 0-88132-128-1	396 pp.

Foreign Direct Investment in the United States
Edward M. Graham and Paul R. Krugman/*1989, 2d ed. October 1991*

ISBN paper 0-88132-139-7	200 pp.

International Adjustment and Financing: The Lessons of 1985-1991
C. Fred Bergsten, editor/*January 1992*

ISBN paper 0-88132-112-5	336 pp.

North American Free Trade: Issues and Recommendations
Gary Clyde Hufbauer and Jeffrey J. Schott/*April 1992*

ISBN cloth 0-88132-145-1	392 pp.
ISBN paper 0-88132-120-6	392 pp.

American Trade Politics
I. M. Destler/*1986, 2d ed. June 1992*

ISBN cloth 0-88132-164-8	400 pp.
ISBN paper 0-88132-188-5	400 pp.

Narrowing the U.S. Current Account Deficit
Allen J. Lenz/*June 1992*

ISBN cloth 0-88132-148-6	640 pp.
ISBN paper 0-88132-103-6	640 pp.

The Economics of Global Warming
William R. Cline/*June 1992*

ISBN cloth 0-88132-150-8	416 pp.
ISBN paper 0-88132-132-X	416 pp.

U.S. Taxation of International Income: Blueprint for Reform
Gary Clyde Hufbauer, assisted by Joanna M. van Rooij/*October 1992*

ISBN cloth 0-88132-178-8	304 pp.
ISBN paper 0-88132-134-6	304 pp.

Who's Bashing Whom? Trade Conflict in High-Technology Industries
Laura D'Andrea Tyson/*November 1992*

ISBN cloth 0-88132-151-6	352 pp.
ISBN paper 0-88132-106-0	352 pp.

Currencies and Politics in the United States, Germany, and Japan
C. Randall Henning/*September 1994*
   ISBN paper 0-88132-127-3   432 pp.

Estimating Equilibrium Exchange Rates
John Williamson, editor/*September 1994*
   ISBN paper 0-88132-076-5   320 pp.

Managing the World Economy: Fifty Years After Bretton Woods
Peter B. Kenen, editor/*September 1994*
   ISBN paper 0-88132-212-1   448 pp.

Reciprocity and Retaliation in U.S. Trade Policy
Thomas O. Bayard and Kimberly Ann Elliott/*September 1994*
   ISBN paper 0-88132-084-6   528 pp.

The Uruguay Round: An Assessment
Jeffrey J. Schott, assisted by Johanna W. Buurman/*November 1994*
   ISBN paper 0-88132-206-7   240 pp.

Measuring the Costs of Protection in Japan
Yoko Sazanami, Shujiro Urata, and Hiroki Kawai/*January 1995* 96 pp.
   ISBN paper 0-88132-211-3

SPECIAL REPORTS

1 Promoting World Recovery: A Statement on Global Economic Strategy
  by Twenty-six Economists from Fourteen Countries/*December 1982*
  (out of print)   ISBN paper 0-88132-013-7   45 pp.

2 Prospects for Adjustment in Argentina, Brazil, and Mexico:
  Responding to the Debt Crisis
  John Williamson, editor/*June 1983*
  (out of print)   ISBN paper 0-88132-016-1   71 pp.

3 Inflation and Indexation: Argentina, Brazil, and Israel
  John Williamson, editor/*March 1985*
          ISBN paper 0-88132-037-4   191 pp.

4 Global Economic Imbalances
  C. Fred Bergsten, editor/*March 1986*
          ISBN cloth 0-88132-038-2   126 pp.
          ISBN paper 0-88132-042-0   126 pp.

5 African Debt and Financing
  Carol Lancaster and John Williamson, editors/*May 1986*
  (out of print)   ISBN paper 0-88132-044-7   229 pp.

6 Resolving the Global Economic Crisis: After Wall Street
  Thirty-three Economists from Thirteen Countries/*December 1987*
          ISBN paper 0-88132-070-6   30 pp.

7 World Economic Problems
  Kimberly Ann Elliott and John Williamson, editors/*April 1988*
          ISBN paper 0-88132-055-2   298 pp.

  Reforming World Agricultural Trade
  Twenty-nine Professionals from Seventeen Countries/*1988*
          ISBN paper 0-88132-088-9   42 pp.

8 Economic Relations Between the United States and Korea:
  Conflict or Cooperation?
  Thomas O. Bayard and Soo-Gil Young, editors/*January 1989*
          ISBN paper 0-88132-068-4   192 pp.

FORTHCOMING

The Globalization of Industry and National Governments
C. Fred Bergsten and Edward M. Graham

The Political Economy of Korea–United States Cooperation
C. Fred Bergsten and Il SaKong, editors

International Debt Reexamined
William R. Cline

Trade, Jobs, and Income Distribution
William R. Cline

American Trade Politics, Third Edition
I. M. Destler

Environment in the New World Order
Daniel C. Esty

Overseeing Global Capital Markets
Morris Goldstein and Peter Garber

Foreign Direct Investment in the United States, Third Edition
Edward M. Graham and Paul R. Krugman

Global Competition Policy
Edward M. Graham and J. David Richardson

Toward a Pacific Economic Community?
Gary Clyde Hufbauer and Jeffrey J. Schott

The Economics of Korean Unification
Marcus Noland

Managing Official Export Credits
John Ray

The Case for Trade: A Modern Reconsideration
J. David Richardson

The Future of the World Trading System
John Whalley, in collaboration with Colleen Hamilton

For orders outside the US and Canada please contact:
Longman Group UK Ltd.
PO Box 88
Fourth Avenue
Harlow, Essex CM 19 5SR
UK

Telephone Orders: 0279 623923
Fax: 0279 453450
Telex: 81259

Canadian customers can order from the Institute or from either:

RENOUF BOOKSTORE	LA LIBERTÉ
1294 Algoma Road	3020 chemin Sainte-Foy
Ottawa, Ontario K1B 3W8	Quebec G1X 3V6
Telephone: (613) 741-4333	Telephone: (418) 658-3763
Fax: (613) 741-5439	Fax: (800) 567-5449